A WELSH COUNTY AT WAR

This original study of Ceredigion and the First World War locates the county and its people in the context of one of the major international upheavals of the twentieth century. The book reveals in illuminating and sometimes surprising detail the many different aspects of life in the county – civilian and military, urban and rural – in the years immediately before the outbreak of war and during the conflict itself. Meticulously researched and written in an accessible style, the book will be read profitably by anyone interested in how world events can change the lives of ordinary people.

PROF. PAUL O'LEARY
SIR JOHN WILLIAMS PROFESSOR OF
WELSH HISTORY, ABERYSTWYTH UNIVERSITY

A WELSH COUNTY AT WAR

ESSAYS ON CEREDIGION AT THE TIME OF THE FIRST WORLD WAR

GWYN JENKINS

i Taliesin Dafydd a Lili Haf

First impression: 2021

© Copyright Gwyn Jenkins and Y Lolfa Cyf., 2021

The publishers wish to acknowledge the support of the Books Council of Wales

Cover image courtesy of Howard C Jones
Cover design: Tanwen Haf

ISBN: 978 1 78461 969 5

Published and printed in Wales
on paper from well-maintained forests by
Y Lolfa Cyf., Talybont, Ceredigion SY24 5HE
website www.ylolfa.com
e-mail ylolfa@ylolfa.com
tel 01970 832 304
fax 832 782

Contents

Acknowledgements

IN RESEARCHING THIS book, I have benefitted from the patient and efficient service for which the staff of the National Library of Wales are renowned, and also from the aid of the perennially cheerful and equally efficient staff of Ceredigion Archives. I am grateful to my friends Iwan M Jones, for commenting on some of the chapters, and Professor Paul O'Leary, who read a draft of the completed book. I have had many useful chats about the war with another old friend, Gilbert Jones. Any errors of fact or interpretation are, of course, my own.

I was delighted that Y Lolfa agreed to publish this book, with the support of the Books Council of Wales. Lefi Gruffudd has, as usual, been particularly helpful and Carolyn Hodges's invaluable editorial work has been to her usual exemplary standard.

As ever, I am grateful to my wife Fal for her patient support. I have dedicated this book to my two grandchildren, Taliesin Dafydd and Lili Haf. Although too young to read it, I hope they will do so in years to come and remember their Dacu with affection.

The royalties from this book will be donated to the Jubilee Storehouse, the food bank in my home village of Penparcau. In my view, there should be no need for food banks in a civilised society.

Gwyn Jenkins
Tal-y-bont
June 2021

Introduction

MY PEOPLE WAS the title of a notorious book published during the First World War, which professed to reveal the true nature of rural society in Ceredigion. At the time of its publication in 1915, it caused an outcry among the people of the county – and in Wales in general – who considered it to be an inaccurate and malicious portrait, depicting a narrowly religious and ignorant society. The book's author, Caradoc Evans, was treated as a pariah in the county of his birth.

Today most critics see the book as no more than a literary work of the imagination, comparable to the writings of James Joyce and his followers, rather than an attempt to analyse social life in Ceredigion at that time in an objective manner. Caradoc Evans certainly concentrated on the dark side and, although the historian Russell Davies has shown that there was some truth in the depiction of the county's society, it was certainly far from being a rounded picture.

As a Cardi born and bred, this book is also about 'my people'. It is my perspective on the county's people of a hundred years ago but, unlike Caradoc Evans's book, it is based on detailed historical research rather than imagination (many would say that I have no imagination!). It is not an attempt to record chronologically the history of the county during the First World War but rather to examine the views and experiences of some individuals and the community in general, in the hope that this will throw some light on the nature of society at that time.

This book is not a military history and, although some soldiers appear, it is more about their relationship with 'their people' back home, rather than their wretched lives in the mud of Flanders or in the searing heat of the Middle East, where many men from the county served. There are no 'heroes' in this book, only men, women and children trying to come to terms with a horrific war which shaped and sometimes destroyed their lives.

*

My interest in the First World War dates from the early 1960s when I watched, on black-and-white television, the fascinating documentary series *The Great War*. It is still a classic of its genre and is worth revisiting– it can now be seen online on YouTube. At university I read *The Deluge*, Arthur Marwick's pioneering study of the effect of a 'total war' on Britain, which threw a different light on social developments at that time, and the expansion of state intervention into the lives of ordinary people. Many years later, I was commissioned to write a book on Wales and the First World War which appeared in 2014. *Cymry'r Rhyfel Byd Cyntaf* ['The Welsh in the First World War'] was the result of many hours of research and although this book ostensibly has a much narrower scope, the groundwork undertaken at that time was invaluable. I also discovered more by working as a researcher on the BBC Radio Cymru documentary series *Cymru 1914–1918*, expertly produced by Dinah Jones's company Silin.

I was subsequently advised to turn my attention away from that war to less depressing subjects, but I felt there was still much to be said and interpretations revisited. Although I concentrate on one particular county in this book, I consider it to have a much wider relevance.

I have used the name 'Ceredigion' in this book – rather than the old name 'Cardiganshire' (or Sir Aberteifi, the name in Welsh at that time) – as this has been the official name of the county for nearly fifty years. Only some of those of older generations remain attached to the former county name. References to the college, now known as Aberystwyth University but for many years as the University College of Wales (UCW) Aberystwyth, posed a more difficult problem. I have used 'Aberystwyth College' or 'the College' and 'Principal', which were the terms commonly used a hundred years ago. (My father, who was first employed at the 'College' in the early 1930s, used 'coll' and 'prini' when not on official business.)

I have not included footnotes, as they tend to disrupt the flow of the narrative, but at the back of the book I have included a detailed section on sources.

*

In March 1917 the poet and academic T Gwynn Jones (see Chapter IV) wrote to a friend, stating:

> What would be interesting would be to return to the Earth in a century's time and read the history of these years. [translation]

Whether T Gwynn Jones, undoubtedly resting in a safe refuge in heaven, is able to read this book or not, it will – hopefully – provide some enlightenment to him and to anyone else seeking to understand some aspects of life in this county a hundred years ago.

I

Preparing for War

To maintain peace, be prepared for war.
LADY HILLS-JOHNES, JULY 1910

CEREDIGION IS A county of 688 square miles, stretching from the Teifi Valley in the south to the southern side of the Dyfi Valley in the north. To the east lies the mountainous area known as Elenydd, while the seas of Cardigan Bay patrol a western border of 52 miles of coastland. It is a county which has never been economically wealthy but is, nevertheless, rich in character and history.

Certainly the Ceredigion of a hundred years ago could hardly be described as possessing a thriving economy. The population, which stood at 59,000 in 1911, had been decreasing since the last years of the nineteenth century – largely as a result of the decline, from the 1880s onwards, of the lead-mining industry in the north of the county, leaving agriculture as the lifeblood of the economy and the main source of employment. Many young men migrated (some temporarily) to south Wales to seek work in the coal-mining industry. Robert Hughes from Llanilar, for example, left the village during the 1870s to work in the pits but by the 1880s had taken his wife and children to Treorchy, where they settled into the vibrant community of the Rhondda.

Ceredigion's largest towns, Aberystwyth and Lampeter, though still small in comparison to other towns in Wales, were sustained to some extent by the presence of universities. Aberystwyth also relied on a large influx of holidaymakers during the summer months to boost its economy.

Social life tended to be centred on chapel and church, although, as we shall see, this was not always the case in Aberystwyth and some other towns. The county's Nonconformist chapels could boast over 40,000 members and *gwrandawyr* ['listeners'], who were attendees but not members, while church communicants totalled about 9,000. These figures, gathered in 1905 at the time of a religious revival, were probably exaggerated but they still indicate a stronger support for Christian worship in the county than in most other parts of Wales.

According to the 1911 census, 89.6% of the county's inhabitants could speak Welsh. Almost all the people living in rural parts could speak the language; however, 25% of the population of Aberystwyth could speak only English, a distinction which is worth bearing in mind in assessing the response of the population to the war.

This anglicisation of Aberystwyth was partly due to the influx of English speakers to the university, but also because of expanding business circles. The situation was exacerbated by an education system in which English was the main means of communication in Aberystwyth schools. One hour a week only was reserved for the teaching of Welsh. It is not surprising, then, that increasingly the means of communication in the town – outside, that is, of the chapels and hearth – in the early decades of the twentieth century, was English. The wider distribution of English-language newspapers, the mass media of the day, also played its part.

The changing nature of Aberystwyth can also be seen in the attitude towards temperance. It was claimed that the town's branches of the Band of Hope, a social organisation for young people organised by the chapels and which promoted temperance, could boast a thousand members at the turn of the century. Certainly the 14 Nonconformist chapels in the town expected abstinence from their members, yet it was reported in 1908 that there were also 47 licensed premises where alcohol could be served. Some of these catered for tourists, but clearly there were many townsfolk who were not averse to drinking intoxicants. These included not only working men who enjoyed a pint of beer in their local but also members of the middle class, who frequented hotels and social clubs.

One particular dispute in 1912 suggests that temperance was no longer a dominant force in the town. In 1911 a golf course was established on the Bryn-y-môr Estate overlooking the town, where it is still spectacularly located. Among its early members were at least two local Methodist ministers (R J Rees and Maurice Griffiths), but others who were prominent in the club sought to allow alcohol to be served in the new clubhouse, built in 1912. There was an attempt by some members, led by R J Rees, to reverse a decision by the club committee to sell alcohol at the club but this was defeated in a straight vote of members. R J Rees commented in his diary: 'The issue has roused [the] town: and has placed some between two stools with the consequent fall [from grace].' The discord was even more pronounced in Maurice Griffiths's own chapel, Salem, as the captain and Chairman of the golf club was Professor Edward Edwards, a Sunday School teacher at the chapel.

What is clear is that the façade of a town where temperance was the norm had been severely cracked. The same might be said of some of the smaller towns. Tregaron, for example, was described in 1916 by one commentator as one of the most 'untemperancelike' in the county:

Not often, I presume, can one see so many inns in such a small place, and these would not be able to carry on with this trade were it not for regular and keen customers. [translation]

Yet temperance remained prevalent in rural areas of the county. Although most substantial villages had inns, community life in rural Ceredigion largely revolved around the chapel and also age-old agricultural practices such as the co-operation of farmers at harvest time or in sheep shearing. Villages might also hold an annual eisteddfod and an agricultural or horticultural show, while some boasted thriving literary and debating societies. In November 1908 the newly formed Llanilar Literary and Debating Society could boast seventy members and lively debates were held on a monthly basis, with their content suggesting a degree of sophistication not often associated with rural communities. Welsh was the predominant language of these activities, except where the benevolence of the local monoglot English gentry was required.

Most of the population was law-abiding, although petty session records point to some drunkenness and pilfering in rural villages and small towns, together with the adulteration of milk by some farmers.

The county was changing slowly as a result of general social and economic forces, but the advent of war was to accelerate some of these changes.

*

Before the war, Ceredigion was believed by many to be imbued with the spirit of peacemaking, rooted in firm Nonconformist religious beliefs. The great symbol of this was Henry Richard, known as 'Apostol Heddwch' ['the Apostle of Peace'], who had campaigned in the nineteenth century for the peaceful resolution of international disputes. An estimated 2,000 people assembled at his birthplace, Tregaron, in August 1893 to witness the unveiling of an impressive statue of him in the town square. Of these, it was claimed that about a thousand had travelled from all parts of Wales and beyond, while the remainder came from Ceredigion.

Presentation of the Colours to the 4th Battalion of the Welsh Regiment, Aberystwyth, 1910

Seventeen years later, a similar-sized crowd attended another quite different ceremony, this time in Aberystwyth. On Saturday, 30 July 1910, the presentation of colours to the 4th Battalion of the Welsh Regiment took place at the College Athletic Grounds (now known as Vicarage Field) in what was described as a 'brilliant and inspiring military spectacle'. The presentation was made by Lieutenant-General Sir James Hills-Johnes GCB, VC and Lady Elizabeth Hills-Johnes, of Dolaucothi. *The Cambrian News* reported:

Addressing the Battalion, Lady Hills-Johnes said that she and Sir James had the greatest pleasure in presenting the colours because they were sure the Battalion would be true to the traditions of the Welsh Regiment and that they would carry the colours with the same honour and courage that had distinguished Welsh soldiers on many a battle field. The Battalion had the privilege of serving this great country not only in war, but in peace, because, to repeat a time-worn truth never too often repeated, "to maintain peace, be prepared for war." By their voluntary act of national service they laid the foundation of peace. If peace were disturbed by outsiders,

15

the Battalion was doubtless ready to defend the right, even at the cost of life itself. Their Honorary Colonel, Sir James Hills-Johnes, would present the Battalion with the regimental colour. It was her honour to present it with the colour bearing the King's cypher and the time-honoured Union Jack. May the battalion long and loyally serve under them and remember the three old Welsh proverbs: '*meistr pob gwaith – ymarfer*'; '*goreu arf – gwroldeb*', and '*goreu tarian – cyfiawnder*' which in English meant, 'master of all work – practice'; 'the best of weapons – courage'; and 'the best shield – righteousness'.

Following the ceremony, at a banquet at Alexandra Hall attended by officers and local dignitaries, General Francis Lloyd – General Officer Commanding the Welsh Division, Territorial Force – stated:

> The dragon of Wales must not sleep. She may rest; but her claws must be sharp, and that can only be attained by our united effort to recruit and to train. Then she may rest and rest trained, and should the enemy have the temerity and assurance to land on these shores, she will arise and stand defiant – not only defensive, but defiant to wield the counter-stroke of the flashing sword of vengeance.

*

Although few, if any, of the attendees at this ceremony in Aberystwyth were also likely to have been at the unveiling of the statue at Tregaron 17 years earlier, the event demonstrated a much more militaristic spirit which had become prevalent among some sections of the population. Though some of the crowd on the bank above the field were probably on holiday in the town, there is abundant evidence that there was widespread support for the event and for the Army in general. Although the percentage of Welshmen in the Regular Army before the war was lower than that of the other nations of the United Kingdom, large numbers of young men had joined the part-time Territorial Army or the Special Army Reserve, which had been established following the Army reforms of 1907.

At the same time, the perceived threat from an expansionist Germany coupled with the glorification of the British Empire, not least in schools, led to this growing militaristic spirit and with it, an expectation of war. This spirit was largely centred in the urban areas of the county and among the local gentry, as was the case in most parts of Britain. It was not necessarily a spirit which welcomed warfare as a means of settling disputes, but was rather rooted in a belief that it was necessary to be prepared to defend one's country, community and family. Such an approval of military defence allowed even those who might have been expected to disapprove of warfare to embrace the armed forces as a necessary response to perceived threats. This was particularly true in the support for the Territorial Army, which had been formed in 1908 essentially as a defensive force, made up of part-time soldiers recruited locally.

In fact the ceremony on Vicarage Field coincided with somewhere between 15,000 and 20,000 members of the Territorial Army (often known as 'Terriers') from all parts of Wales and the Marches arriving in the county by train, and encamping at Lovesgrove on the outskirts of Aberystwyth and in fields near Bow Street. This was the largest military presence in Ceredigion since the days of Henry Tudor or Owain Glyndŵr, several centuries earlier. As one diarist noted: 'The whole country flocked there to see them and there was a great deal of rowdyism.'

At the end of July 1910 the 'Terriers' participated in military manoeuvres in which a section of the Army pretended to be an invading force landing in the Dyfi Valley while another force sought to repel them in the hills to the north of Aberystwyth. The residents of the small village of Bont-goch considered the mock battles to be very realistic and the events were described in detail in the local press:

> The mountains reverberated with the din of canonading, the rattle
> of the maxim, and the crack of the rifle, but with the exception
> of small groups of men leaping a fence or crossing a field, the
> combatants were out of sight, until the operations were over
> and the signals were given to show the positions attained, when
> the whole countryside was seen covered with khaki-clothed
> Territorials.

There was very little opposition to these military exercises in this allegedly pacifist county. A prominent Methodist from Anglesey, the Revd T C Williams (later an active Army recruiter), conducted a joint service with an Anglican counterpart in the Territorials' camp at Bow Street in 1910, and among the men of the cloth participating at the presentation of the colours ceremony was the Revd T E Roberts, the Methodist Minister of Seilo Chapel, Aberystwyth. Ironically, during the same week, he had been a staunch critic of a boxing 'carnival' which was to be held in the town's Skating Rink pavilion. Clearly only certain forms of fighting were acceptable.

Concerns were expressed locally about the potential danger of drunken soldiers roaming the streets of Aberystwyth and there were fears that local young women might be attracted to, or seduced by, men in uniform, but the visit of such a large military force proved to be largely uneventful for the local population. Indeed local businesses, including cab drivers, food suppliers and post offices, benefitted from these large camps and they seem not to have prevented holidaymakers from visiting the area in high numbers. A contemporary survey recorded that the number of visitors to Aberystwyth in the summer of 1910 exceeded 11,000, and that in a borough with a resident population of fewer than 8,000 people.

*

There is some isolated evidence of opposition to this militarism from the chapel members in Aberystwyth, but it was also the case that religious services for the military were held in some Nonconformist chapels, as well as in the Anglican churches. In mid July 1910 *The Welsh Gazette* reported that: 'the local corps of Territorials marched to Tabernacle Chapel on Sunday morning last for their first parade after camp. The Rev. R. J. Rees, M.A., pastor, delivered an eloquent sermon, the service being in English.'

R J Rees also chaired a meeting of the Tabernacl Literary and Debating Society in February 1912, at which a debate was held on whether churches should support the Territorials, the Boys' Brigade, the Boy Scouts and similar organisations. The motion was opposed by Dewi Morgan, the well-known poet-journalist, and John Jenkins but 'the affirmative was carried by a handsome majority'.

Rees was also to speak during the following month at a meeting of the South Wales Calvinistic Methodist Association in which the movement of troops and musketry practice by the Territorials on Sundays was virulently opposed. He said:

> It was with very great difficulty that the Territorial organisation had placed itself in keeping with Welsh national sentiment. There was a love of peace in Wales. The trade of a soldier had not always been a trade that even they, as Nonconformists, had been in favour of. Many of them today, in the responsibility of their citizenship, had been prepared to support the formation of a land army of this kind for the defence of their own shores, but if that meant bringing about the desecration of the Sabbath in Wales it would throw into the ranks of those who opposed the Territorial movement, every one of them who in days gone by thought a movement of this kind had something to be said for it.

It is clear that, in his eyes, the fourth commandment trumped the sixth.

The chapels did not discourage the establishment of semi-militaristic youth organisations. Although the Boy Scout groups formed after the Boer War were not military organisations as such, they did involve youths coming together to go camping and undertake physical exercises. Many of its early members would undoubtedly have been the first to enlist with the Army in 1914. This would also have been true of the semi-militaristic Boys' Brigade, an organisation originally founded in 1883 'to combine drill and fun activities with Christian values.' By 1909 the Aberystwyth branch of the Boys' Brigade had over 70 members, while the Cardigan Boy Scouts had a 28-member Fife and Drum Band.

A Church Lads' Brigade was also set up in Aberystwyth in 1908, with the vicar of St Michael's Church stating: 'Now, this brigade was formed in order to bring together all Church lads, to learn [sic] them obedience, to be better men, and fitter Churchmen. Every member of the brigade must be a member of a Church or some Church organisation, and they must stick loyally to that principle.'

While the Territorials were exercising in the area in July 1910, a 'sham fight' was arranged in Aberystwyth between the amalgamated forces of the three local corps of Boy Scouts, Boys' Brigade and Church Lads' Brigade. The parties were divided into attacking and defending forces. The manoeuvres were carried out on the banks behind the National School (above North Road), and, according to press reports, '...proved very exciting, the boys entering with much gusto into the operations'.

Also on parade in Aberystwyth in the years before the war was the College's Officer Training Corps. The OTC, which was formed in 1908, was led by Professor Jimmy Marshall and annually attracted as many as 80 young male students, a considerable number in a college where the total number of male students was about 250 at that time. Many of the members of the OTC were to become commissioned officers in 1914 and, during the war, suffered from the very high casualty rate among subalterns.

The maritime tradition of the county led to many seamen joining the Royal Naval Reserve. They received a retainer paid by the Admiralty and would spend one month a year undertaking gunnery training on drill-ships. There were over 40 members of the Aberystwyth District of the RNR in 1914 and *The Cambrian News* reported that 84 Aberystwyth men went to sea at the outbreak of war. In Cardigan and St Dogmaels, local Naval Reservists known as *'Bois y Batri'* [the Battery Boys] had been training for many years at Glanteifi on the Teifi Estuary. Although this site had closed in 1906, about 60 members of the local RNR were among the first to be called up in 1914.

Undoubtedly all these organisations provided a more exhilarating environment for young men than that which they might have experienced at the Band of Hope, the main organisation for young people in Ceredigion at the turn of the century. Nevertheless, these were organisations centred in the larger towns, while rural areas – apart, that is, from the mansions of the gentry – were largely immune to the overtly militaristic spirit on show in the urban parts of the county. Of the 140 members of the Cardiganshire Battery with Ceredigion addresses on 1 August 1914, only 10% came from outside the borough of Aberystwyth, while of the 83 members of the 4th Battery of the Welsh Regiment based at Cardigan, only 9 had addresses from outside of that town.

Considering the military preparations undertaken during the early years of the century, it is not surprising that the people of Ceredigion, most notably its urban population, did not follow the tradition symbolised by Henry Richard when war was declared in August 1914. Rather, as General Francis Lloyd had claimed in 1910, the Welsh dragon would 'stand defiant... to wield the counter-stroke of the flashing sword of vengeance.'

II

Waiting on the Lord: Response and Recruitment

Dowch gyda mi, fechgyn! [Come with me, boys!]

RECRUITMENT POSTER

I see lots of young, strong, able-bodied
men who have no intention of volunteering,
and no leaders to seek them.

LETTER TO THE *WESTERN MAIL*, OCTOBER 1914

TWO FASCINATING PHOTOGRAPHS of events in Aberystwyth following the declaration of war in August 1914 have survived. In one photograph two prominent local Territorial officers are to be seen in a train compartment at Aberystwyth station on 10 August, ready to leave for war. Major (later Lieutenant Colonel) J C (Jack) Rea was a former Welsh International footballer and the son of the proprietor of the White Horse, a wine merchant, grocery business and public house which still stands in Terrace Road. The other was Dr Abraham Thomas, the local Medical Officer of Health, who was promoted to the rank of major during the war. Rea led the Cardiganshire Battery, 2nd Welsh Brigade, Royal Field Artillery (the local branch of the Territorials), while Thomas acted as its surgeon.

Territorial officers ready to leave Aberystwyth, August 1914. In the compartment: Major Jack Rea and Major Abraham Thomas. On the platform: unknown officer, D C Roberts, Vaughan Davies MP
(courtesy of Howard C Jones)

Local soldiers leaving Aberystwyth with a crowd of well-wishers, August 1914
(courtesy of Howard C Jones)

Wishing them well on the platform were Councillor (later Sir) D C Roberts, one of the most influential figures in the town; Matthew Vaughan-Davies (later Lord Ystwyth), the county's Member of Parliament; and another Territorial officer.

Another photograph taken at the station on the same day shows cheerful soldiers from the ranks of the Cardiganshire Battery, surrounded by well-wishers from the town. These young Territorials, about 150 in number, had met up earlier at the Drill Hall, Aberystwyth – which, if descriptions of other similar events are to be believed, would have been a more sombre occasion, with family members in tears and an air of trepidation prevailing. Only the most naive of recruits would not have realised that they might never return. However, outside there were smiling faces and an atmosphere of excitement as the young men went to war and an uncertain fate.

There are also photographs from other parts of the county from the same period, most notably a striking image of the Lampeter contingent of Yeomanry riding across the bridge over the Teifi on their way to Carmarthen to join up with other colleagues from west Wales. In October, it was reported that some 43 members of the Cardiganshire Yeomanry Squadron had enlisted and were soon to be attached to the Pembrokeshire Yeomanry, which was heading to a camp in Norfolk for training. In November, it was claimed in the press that, in all, 108 men from the county had joined the Yeomanry, mainly from the Lampeter and Llanybydder area, though a few came from villages further afield such as Lledrod and Bow Street.

Another photograph shows a train leaving Cardigan carrying local members of the Royal Naval Reserve, who were called up at the same time as the Territorials. It was reported that 41 Naval Reservists from the town had been called up, together with a further 44 from the Aberystwyth District. Many years later, one Naval Reservist, Dick Arfon Jones, a well-known character in Aberystwyth, recalled his march with the Reservists along the prom in August 1914 before they left

Cardiganshire Yeomanry leaving Lampeter, August 1914

by night train for Liverpool. He said: 'I wondered how many would return – many did not.'

Also enlisting were members of the Aberystwyth College Officer Training Corps, most of whom were seeking commissions. By 1915 the number of students then enrolled at the College who were serving with the armed forces was 85.

These young men clearly had the support of the majority of the county's townspeople and there was no overt opposition to the conflict, despite the sudden lurch to war which had taken many by surprise. This positive attitude, which was at its most evident in the county's main towns, was likely to provide a fruitful source of recruitment to the armed forces over the ensuing months.

*

The response in rural areas was somewhat different. Very few of the Territorials lived in rural areas, and, although some rural horsemen joined the Yeomanry, there was no explicit enthusiasm for war outside the towns – except, that is, from

25

among the landed gentry. Indeed many rural families, which tended to be close-knit and suspicious of external influences, were anxious that their sons did not enlist.

In Llanilar in August 1914, two conmen (one of whom was later gaoled) pretended to be Army recruiting officers and found it rather easy to trick parents into paying them to keep their sons from being called up. Clearly there was no war enthusiasm among those ready to pay to avoid the call to fight 'for King and country'.

Mothers were particularly protective of their sons. Recruiting agents were largely unsuccessful at the annual hiring fair at Aberystwyth, as reported in the local press:

> When approached by a recruiting agent who was in uniform, one young man referred the officer to his mother, who immediately held up her hands in horror. It was stated that this woman had three sturdy sons, none of whom had enlisted. The general excuse of the young men was that they were willing to join the army when compelled to do so.

It is clear too that Dafydd Jones's mother, Margaret Jones of Wern Isaf Farm near Llanddewi Brefi, was adamant that he should not seek to enlist. When he, an Aberystwyth College student, did so, he wrote home to apologise profusely to her for acting against her wishes. Likewise W Jones-Edwards of Ffair Rhos, who enlisted sometime later, stated in his memoirs:

> When I told my story [that he had enlisted], poor Mam nearly broke her heart and my father went dumb. My sisters and brothers did not know what to say, and there is no need to guess what the reaction of my grandmother and aunt was. [translation]

It was also claimed at the time by one local councillor that, as a means of avoiding military service, the number of Aberystwyth students from farming backgrounds increased significantly after 1914:

This is a terrible war and we have all our work cut out to get through it. I am sorry to say that there are a number of 'slackers' in this country, there are about 60 farmers sons, back at the college, the largest number ever known. In fact there never has been more than 30 previous to this session, it is simply an excuse to shirk enlisting but by God we will have the Devils out of the town.

There were complaints in the press about the failure to recruit young men from the county. G Lloyd Williams of Rhydlewis wrote to the *Western Mail* in October 1914:

I think it would wake Cardiganshire up if you were to call attention to the gross apathy in this county in the war. I find the "heads" doing nothing: no meetings, no committees. What are the magistrates doing? Nothing. I see lots of young, strong, able-bodied men who have no intention of volunteering, and no leaders to seek them. I never in all my life seen [sic] such apathy.

However, this was not entirely true. There had been much understandable disorganisation in the early weeks of the war, but by mid September, following a county meeting at Lampeter, Captain Sir Edward Pryse of Gogerddan was designated the Chief Recruiting Officer for the county and local agents were appointed, covering all parts of the county. A series of recruiting meetings in towns and villages were also arranged.

On 1 October, 'an enthusiastic and largely-attended meeting' was held at Aberaeron, where the Methodist minister, the Revd D Lewis Rees, 'eloquently appealed to young men who were capable of bearing arms to enlist.' Nine young men enlisted following the meeting.

However, meetings held in rural villages were often unsuccessful. Following 'a crowded and enthusiastic meeting' in Llanilar, only three local young men volunteered, while at Llanwenog it was reported that '...As far as actual recruiting is concerned, the meeting bore no immediate result'. It was also reported that '...an enthusiastic and crowded meeting' at Llan-non lasted for two hours but 'in spite of the eloquent appeals made, the enthusiasm failed to cause any desirable candidates to enlist. Three came forward but did not satisfy the standard of measurements.'

The lack of enthusiasm in rural areas was not necessarily a consequence of a pacifist tradition or the result of profound religious beliefs, but was more likely to derive from a reluctance to become involved in distant disputes or to disrupt livelihoods.

*

During the early weeks of the war, the press reported extensively on alleged atrocities by the invading German Army in Belgium, and often the appeals for recruits made at public meetings were framed by the widespread belief that such acts would be repeated were Britain to be invaded by the Germans. Playing on this fear had greater leverage than most other arguments. This was expressed in the aforementioned Dafydd Jones's letter to his mother:

> Please bear in mind that this country is waiting every minute for the Germans to land here. After that we would only be like poor Belgians with their homes torn apart. I think you would rather lose one son than lose the whole family. [translation]

There was also a direct call for men to display their manliness. This was the message of Principal Llewelyn Bebb of St David's College, Lampeter at a meeting which was held in the town in September 1914. He claimed '...that right throughout the country was ringing a tremendous appeal to men to show that they were men.'

Bebb was an Anglican who saw his three sons volunteer at the outbreak of war. Despite the Christian message as expounded by Christ being unequivocally pacifist, the Anglican Church had never found it uncomfortable to fully support what it deemed to be a 'just war'. The war was portrayed in some quarters as a crusade against unchristian behaviour by an aggressive regime, despite the fact that the Germans prayed to the same God in churches not particularly dissimilar to those in Britain.

Anglican ministers supported the war effort by any means possible and were always ready to criticise their Nonconformist neighbours for their perceived failure to back the war and, in particular, to encourage recruitment to the armed services. This was at a time when the long debate over the disestablishment and disendowment of the Anglican Church in Wales had come to a head. It suited Anglicans to find fault with Nonconformists, while fighting a last-ditch attempt to block the passage of the Welsh Church Act 1914, which was scheduled to be put into effect when the war ended.

In the event, many Nonconformist ministers also gave their unconditional support to recruitment and very few openly opposed the war. The role of David Lloyd George, one of the most influential ministers in the Government, in persuading Nonconformist ministers to recruit for the armed forces is often considered to have been crucial in the changing attitude of the Nonconformists from August 1914 onwards. However, many of the Nonconformist ministers who were prominent in Army recruitment were actively recruiting at the immediate outset of the war, and had long since accepted the necessity of the armed services. One of the most prominent recruiters, the Revd T C Williams of Porthaethwy, was a chaplain in the Territorial Army, while the most influential Nonconformist minister in Ceredigion, the Revd R J Rees (of whom more later, in Chapter IV) had expressed support for the Territorial movement in the pre-war years and appeared on recruitment platforms throughout the county.

Only a few Nonconformist ministers openly opposed the war, the most vocal being T E Nicholas (known as 'Niclas y Glais'), who was a minister at Llangybi near Lampeter in 1914 (see Chapter IX). His was largely a lone voice in the county, where most ministers supported the war. Those with genuine misgivings tended to settle for a low profile. The Revd O H Jones, the Minister of Carmel Chapel, Llanilar, was a natural pacifist who used his limited influence to support conscientious objectors, but like many others, he concentrated on providing succour to families in his congregation who had sons or husbands in the Army, rather than speaking out publicly against the war.

The Revd Moelwyn Hughes, the Presbyterian Minister of Tabernacl Chapel in Cardigan, was also a pacifist but did not publicly oppose the war. At the outset of the war, there were rumours that he was pro-German but in sermons preached at Seilo Chapel, Aberystwyth in October 1914, he strongly denounced the actions and attitude of the Kaiser, as well as the barbarous conduct of German soldiers, and called on Britishers to do all in their power to destroy the tyranny of militarism and restore peace in Europe. Later, in a published sermon in March 1915, he quoted Christ's words from the book of Matthew (24:6):

> And you will hear of wars and rumours of wars. See that you are not alarmed, for this must take place, but the end is not yet. For nation will rise against nation, and kingdom against kingdom, and there will be famines and earthquakes in various places. All these are but the beginning of the birth pains.

He preached of his conviction that God would ultimately triumph and that there would soon be another religious revival.

Perhaps the viewpoint of the Revd Maurice Griffiths, the Methodist Minister of Salem, Aberystwyth, encapsulated the attitude of many Nonconformist ministers:

> *Mewn ymostyngiad a gweddi bydded i ninnau ddisgwyl am yr Arglwydd, gan geisio cyfarwyddyd ei ysbryd i ddehongli arwyddion yr amserau, a chymwyso ein hunain ar gyfer problemau ein bywyd.*

['In submission and prayer, let us wait on the Lord, seeking instruction from his spirit to interpret the signs of the times, and apply ourselves for our life's problems.']

'Waiting on the Lord' meant that they avoided tying themselves into theological knots and averted the confusion represented by one deacon from north Wales, who prayed from the *sêt fawr* [the great pew below the pulpit where deacons sit] of a chapel in Llanrwst:

> We know, O Lord, that the Germans also ask for your help to win this war as urgently as we do. But, O Lord, will you remain neutral until we have destroyed them?

*

Apart from visits by Army recruiters and recruitment meetings, efforts to encourage enlistment involved use of the press, distribution of pamphlets and leaflets and placing of posters in prominent locations. Some of the literature was in Welsh, such as the poster of a smiling soldier marching off to war under the slogan *'Dowch gyda mi, fechgyn!'* ['Come with me, boys!'] .

Another method was to hold route marches by soldiers billeted or camping in the area. In January 1915 about a thousand members of the 1st Monmouthshire Regiment marched from Aberystwyth to Tal-y-bont. It was reported in *The Cambrian News* that:

> Everybody admired the fine physique of the men, who in their march showed that they have been efficiently drilled. It was a treat to watch their martial appearance and the promptitude of their movements. The march through Tal-y-bont will have a great influence upon the young men in inducing them to join the colours. The young men who were at drill that evening as special constables were encouraging one another to joined [sic] the army...

31

Army recruitment in Tal-y-bont, 1915

The Monmouths were among the 9,000 soldiers from various regiments billeted in Aberystwyth between December 1914 and July 1915, another means of encouraging enlistment and general support for the war. The billeting also brought with it a boost for the local economy, although there is evidence of some altercations between English and Welsh soldiers, which, according to the Revd R J Rees's diary, led to enforced '...night marches as a measure of punishment & precaution.'

The local press was a useful means of encouraging recruitment. Reports – often with photographs – appeared in the newspapers, chronicling the service given by soldiers at the front and sailors on the high seas. Pride of place was often given to 'patriotic families', such as the photographs of the ten sons and grandsons of the late Thomas Jenkins, builder, Penparcau, which featured in *The Cambrian News* in March 1918.

The press also published letters from soldiers at the front, which often included a call to arms. Among the correspondents was Rifleman Willie Stanley Jones. His family lived on the Buarth, Aberystwyth and, although they were Methodists, he

Recruitment poster: 'Come with me, boys!'

had probably before the war been in the Church Lads' Brigade which met at the Holy Trinity Hall on the Buarth. The Brigade had strong links with the King's Royal Rifles (K.R.R.) and, at the outbreak of war, Jones joined that regiment.

In early 1915 he fought as a Lewis gunner at Givenchy and Festubert, where he was wounded in the foot. From his hospital bed he wrote home, describing, in horrifying detail, these battles and the casualties suffered. Of Givenchy he wrote:

> Over the top go the boys. My God what a sight – they were mown down like ripe corn, on their heels race the second line but the poor chaps were destined to receive the same fate as their comrades being practically wiped out to a man.

Of the night attack at Festubert he wrote that 'the lads... fell and fell and fell', but the K.R.R. attacked again:

> ...for the third time I go over, & I find that I have been hit somewhere in the foot. I rush forward. We get our gun into action – the Germans are on the run, & we let them have it hot, a good old 700 rounds a minute. They are falling over like flies...With daylight the tremendous price of victory came into view – the bodies sprawled & huddled & heaped on the open ground the advance had covered between the trenches. The khaki uniforms showed plainly against the long, green grass or among the streaks & splash of chocolate brown earth thrown up by the ploughing shells, and, more plainly still the eye caught the round black dot of a bare head, the gleam of a white turned up face.

At the end of this letter, he called on local young men to join the Army:

> If there are any Aber boys who have not yet enlisted, you can assure them that they will be welcomed in the ranks of the K.R.R.

What effect this and other similar appeals had on young men is difficult to gauge. Some might have felt a sense of duty to join up, but surely many would have been horrified by the bloody descriptions of the fighting and the considerable casualty rate, leading them to be fearful of falling victim to the carnage so vividly described in the letter.

No doubt it was this second group, often described in letters from the front as 'slackers' or 'shirkers', who understandably avoided enlistment and, when conscription was introduced in 1916, sought exemption.

*

There are no official figures on the number of those recruited and conscripted to the armed forces from Ceredigion during the war. We can calculate (see Appendix) that the total number of those who served was about five and a half thousand men out of an eligible male population of eleven thousand. Of these, it has been estimated that about 44% were likely to have been conscripted or joined up by means of the 'Group scheme' (see Chapter VI) – that is, about two thousand, four hundred men from the county. This means that a little over three thousand men from the county volunteered at some point during the first 18 months of the war or were already in the Regular Army. It is also estimated that about five and a half thousand eligible men did not volunteer and were not conscripted. Some of these would have failed an Army medical, while others would have been exempted from fighting through the Military Service Tribunals. Although those who served were mostly the fittest and strongest men in the county, it is a myth that the county was denuded of all its young men during the war.

III

Dr Ethé: Leaders and Led

The public may rest assured that the great majority of Germans remaining in this country are peaceful and innocent persons from whom no danger is to be feared.

REGINALD MCKENNA, HOME SECRETARY, 10 AUGUST 1914

It was not the hooligans; it was the responsible leaders of the town who did this.

PRINCIPAL T F ROBERTS (R T JENKINS, *EDRYCH YN ÔL*)

THE RAILWAY STATION at Aberystwyth was the busiest location in the town a hundred years ago. There were about 80 employees working there, including booking clerks, porters, train drivers, guards, parcel clerks, tea ladies and newspaper sellers. It was the end of the line for visitors and goods to west Wales and the beginning of journeys out of town towards the rest of Wales, England and beyond. Among the deliveries to the town which came in on the train were a variety of newspapers which, during the war, were read avidly by townspeople anxious to hear the latest news from the front. The station's concourse was therefore a bustling centre for gossip and intrigue, of tearful farewells and joyful welcomes, and with a huge amount of coming and going amid the steam and black smut belching from the engines.

In the late afternoon of 14 October 1914, a number of well-known figures from the town had congregated at the station. Alderman (later Sir) D C Roberts, a highly respected councillor and the town's Mayor at the time, had been to a meeting of the Council of the National Library of Wales held in the Assembly Rooms near St Michael's Church. The Mayor had met up with the College's Principal, T F Roberts, in Great Darkgate Street and they had walked together to the station, where the Mayor intended to buy a newspaper. At the station, T F Roberts was met by the College's Registrar, J H Davies, together with three senior students, who were there to meet a member of the College's professorial staff and escort him to his home. When the train arrived at 5.25 p.m., the German-born professor, Hermann Ethé, and his English wife alighted and were greeted by the Principal and Registrar and soon escorted to their home in Caradog Road. Witnesses to the event deemed it to be an official welcome involving not only the College but also the Mayor.

However, it seems certain that the Mayor was there by coincidence and the purpose of the deputation by the College was to ensure that the professor was escorted to his home as smoothly as possible. This was because the College authorities had been alerted by the Chief Constable that Professor Ethé might be under some threat, emanating from the strong anti-German feeling which was being stirred up in the town. Professor Ethé's return that evening was to lead, on the following day, to one of the most unsavoury incidents in the history of Aberystwyth.

*

College professors were seen by many in Aberystwyth to be a class apart, and none more so than Professor Ethé. He was, by 1914, 70 years old, and had been on the staff of the College since 1875. Apart from his nationality, his eccentricities,

Contemporary cartoon of Professor Ethé by ap Rhobert

his fondness for alcohol, his peculiar gait as he walked the Promenade, as well as his distinctive accent, made him a unique figure in the town. An Aberystwyth councillor once claimed that 'Professors look down with contempt on ordinary mortals and do not associate with them', and, although Ethé was not particularly snobbish, he was certainly perceived as some sort of exotic bird standing apart from the more sombre and staid elements of Aberystwyth.

However, in the College, he was generally popular with staff and students alike and recognised as a scholar of international repute in the field of oriental languages. One former student (R T Jenkins) described him as 'stupendous', a giant of a scholar and a polymath who taught a number of classes, including German. Another student (Gwilym Hywel Jones) told T Gwynn Jones that Ethé's '...enthusiasm and conscientiousness in his work were very great.' It is not surprising, then, that the Principal was anxious to retain his services during the war, despite his nationality.

As was their custom, Ethé and his wife had spent the 1914 summer vacation in Germany, and at the outbreak of war the College had to appeal to the Home Office for special dispensation to allow the professor to return to his duties in Aberystwyth. The situation was made more difficult by the fact that Ethé had not previously sought British citizenship, despite living in Wales for 40 years. This was to be held against him in due course.

On 13 October, the Principal had received a telegram from Ethé, stating that he would be travelling by train to Aberystwyth the following day. This must have become known among some townspeople and the Chief Constable warned the Principal of the burgeoning anti-German feeling in the town. Indeed it had been suggested that Ethé might be met at Borth station, some seven miles north of the town, rather than at Aberystwyth station, and then secretly transported to his home by car. It appears that, after consulting the Chief Constable, the Principal decided against this course of action. In retrospect this may have averted some, though not all, of the incidents which followed.

*

Professor Ethé returned to Aberystwyth at a time of extreme anti-German feeling, endemic not only in the town but in Britain in general. He was one of over 50,000 native Germans resident in Britain at the outbreak of war. The majority lived in London, with perhaps only a dozen living in Ceredigion.

During the early weeks of the war, there had been anti-German riots in London and elsewhere, amid calls for the internment of all 'alien enemies' rather than merely the thousands of German nationals of military service age who had already been interned in detention camps – a measure which mirrored what had happened to British subjects in Germany. All aliens (foreign nationals) were instructed to register with the authorities and those that did not were fined. There was also a widespread search for spies, and several innocent travellers were arrested based on the unfounded suspicions of over-vigilant members of the public. Such suspicions were no doubt aroused by films such as *The German Spy Peril*, shown at cinemas throughout the country – including Cheetham's Cinema, Aberystwyth. In Aberystwyth a local painter and decorator was reported to the police as a suspected spy as he was seen making notes outside a building. He was in fact taking details for a potential work tender.

The right-wing press, notably the *Daily Mail* and the *Evening News*, launched campaigns against German employees in London hotels and restaurants and the public were urged to boycott any establishments employing enemy aliens. Throughout Britain, many individual Germans, whether registered or not, were identified by local people and pressed to leave their homes. In the small town of Llanrwst, a large crowd assembled to rid the Conwy Valley of a German hotel manager amid cries of *"I'r afon â fo!"* ['To the river with him!'].

A similar attitude was prevalent in Aberystwyth, as its townspeople came to terms with what they perceived to be a desperate battle for survival against a barbarian foe. The town had witnessed many of its young Territorial soldiers and

Naval Reservists head off to war in August 1914 and scores of volunteers had enlisted subsequently, most notably in September 1914 when Army voluntary recruitment was at its highest. From the outset, local and national newspapers carried reports of fierce fighting, coupled with long lists of casualties, which had become an object of great concern locally. In a small town, almost everyone knew of a family which had sons, husbands or brothers in uniform and it was natural to seek to support them by any means possible.

Some overt demonstration of support was possible. When Private Llewelyn George Hicks returned home in late September 1914, having been wounded in action in the first major battle of the war at Mons, he was given a civic welcome at the station by the Mayor, the College Principal and other prominent townspeople. He was, according to *The Welsh Gazette*:

> ...taken on a triumphal march through the town. A procession was formed headed by the local police ...and followed by a large squad of the Special police, commanded by Sgt Major Fear. Martial music was supplied by the Boys Brigade bugle band... The carriage was surrounded by a number of standard bearers who carried large Union Jacks and other national flags... Townspeople turned out in their hundreds and gave the brave soldier a most enthusiastic reception.

A similar reception was afforded to a contingent of Belgian refugees who arrived in the town in early October, as reported in *The Cambrian News*:

> The Station precincts were crowded and the visitors were cheered on making their appearance. The majority of them were women and children, some of the children being orphans... the Boy Scouts assisted in removing the luggage to the Queen's Hotel [at the north end of the Prom]. In the evening a large crowd of students and townspeople assembled in front of the hotel and the visitors joined in singing the national anthems.

The Belgians brought with them tales of German atrocities which easily fanned the flames of anti-German feelings already prevalent in the town. This was reinforced by the publication of the experiences of a local seaman, John Morris of Portland Street, who had been detained in Germany in late July. He had been the mate of a Cardiff steamer, *Glyndŵr*, which was shipping coal to Russia when it was commandeered off the coast of East Prussia. Morris and the crew were badly treated by their captors and were marched off to prison in front of jeering crowds. A fellow crew-member, Alfred Perrett from Cardiff, related his story to the *Western Mail* and this was reproduced in *The Welsh Gazette* and *The Cambrian News* once it had been discovered that Morris too was on the ship. According to Perret, members of the crew were given little food and the sanitary arrangements were 'too vile to talk about'. While on a subsequent train journey to Stettin (Szczecin, Poland), the train stopped at Koning (Chojnice, Poland):

> Our carriage drew up opposite a tap on the station platform. On the platform were a number of male and female Red Cross nurses. We beseeched them to give us some water. What they did was to spit on our faces, jeer us, and turn on the tap to tantalise us. It was seven o'clock on the following morning when we got to Stettin, and we had then been thirty-eight hours since we last had bread and a drink of water.

Morris, Perret and two other members of the crew were, following the intervention of the American Consulate, subsequently released, as they were all over 45 years old and were deemed to be too old to serve in the armed forces. The rest of the crew was, however, interned. *The Cambrian News* reported on 9 October that '...Mr Morris has been heartily congratulated by his friends on his fortunate escape and safe arrival home.'

Those hundreds of townspeople who read in the press of Morris's ill-treatment, together with those who had welcomed the Belgian refugees and Hicks's return from the front, were undoubtedly among those who responded to the call to remove all German residents from the town.

*

Among those who witnessed Ethé's return to Aberystwyth was Enoch Davies, a 43-year-old commercial traveller specialising in grain, who had settled in the town from his native Ruthin some ten years earlier. He lived with his wife, Guiana, and their two children in Trefor Road. He later stated that he had been at the station when Ethé arrived and '...was thunderstruck to notice the welcome accorded to the alien enemy of their country.' Consequently he had approached the Principal and Registrar in the presence of Ethé and remonstrated with them '...as he considered every German an enemy.'

Without doubt, Davies was primarily responsible for organising the demonstration of the following day. This was arranged at such short notice by word of mouth and by the distribution of a leaflet, probably printed by one of the two small local printers in the town. The leaflet simply stated:

> As the protest against the return of Dr Ethé from Germany to teach in our Welsh National Institution, we intend to form a procession of workmen and others at one o'clock to-day near Shiloh [Seilo] chapel.

At the appointed hour, it was reported that about 2,000 townspeople had assembled in the square in front of Seilo Chapel at the end of North Parade (where the Morlan Centre is now). The spontaneous nature of the event is clear. *The Cambrian News* reported that there '...was a mass of men and women standing about in groups and lines with apparently no organising spirit among them... and had no idea how best to demonstrate.' T Gwynn Jones, who was passing by on his way home to lunch, was of the opinion that: 'The crowd was then quite good humoured & a sensible speaker could, I think, have managed them.'

However, there was no plan in place for speakers. Councillor T J Samuel, a local solicitor, was persuaded to address the protesters and as there was no prepared platform, such as a cart, he was hoisted up onto a tree. Confronted by a large, excitable crowd, his off-the-cuff speech included the following statement, as reported in *The Cambrian News*:

> ...he understood that the feeling of the working men of the town and others at the return to Aberystwyth of certain gentlemen who were Germans was one of resentment and that they wanted to express that feeling by a demonstration. That great crowd proved that they were patriotic and that they did not want to see any of their enemies among them. He would be sorry to say a word against a certain gentleman whom they all knew. He had lived among them many years and had not deemed it necessary to become a naturalised British citizen, and that spoke volumes. In that demonstration he hoped that the people of Aberystwyth would act as Britons and do nothing out of place to injure anybody.

The next speaker, Dr T D Harries – also a councillor – was more bellicose. He asked the crowd:

> '...if it wanted any Germans in Aberystwyth? (Cries of "No.") What then were they going to do? ("Shoot them.") Do not let them act like Germans who tore women and children to pieces, but give them twenty-four hours' notice to clear out, and if they were not out of the town by that time, he would lead in turning them out.

Enoch Davies then called on the crowd to march to Ethé's house in Caradog Road. Whether this was premeditated is not clear but once such a large crowd, described in the press as 'ugly and dangerous', had assembled, it was difficult to prevent the more unsavoury events that followed. It was noticeable that, despite the presence of senior police officers, little attempt was made to control the mob elements and T Gwynn Jones thought that Police Superintendent Phillips, with whom he spoke, sympathised with the crowd. It is also likely that any Special Constables present were probably among the protesters.

*

Led by a man carrying a large red ensign flag, the crowd marched up Northgate Street and then turned into Llanbadarn Road before turning left into Caradog Road, where Ethé lived. The crowd trampled on the front garden of the house before Mrs Ethé came to the window, from which she bravely reasoned with the crowd's spokesman, Enoch Davies. She stated that she was English with a brother in the Army and that her husband was not in the house. A woman in the crowd pressed forward and '...excitedly exclaimed that the husband was in the house, but it was just like the Germans to shelter behind women and children.' The message was then conveyed to Mrs Ethé that the professor was to leave the town within 24 hours or, as was shouted by someone in the crowd: '...we will come and pull the house down.'

At that point two other professors arrived at the scene. Professor Marshall was the officer in charge of the College's Officer Training Corps but his status was not sufficient to quell the crowd's temper. He made some uncomplimentary remarks about the misbehaviour he had witnessed and was 'bonneted' – that is, his hat was pressed down over his head – by a protester. Marshall was rescued by Police Superintendent Phillips who, with some difficulty, escorted him and the other professor, O T Jones, away from the baying mob to safety.

Some of the crowd then headed through town to search for other resident Germans. At one point they were berated for their behaviour by a College student, but he was set upon and beaten before being rescued by other students. The message that all Germans were to leave the town was delivered to the Belle Vue and Queen's hotels, where it was claimed some

Germans were employed, and a hairdresser living in Greenfield Street was given the same order.

After Caradog Road, however, the first port of call was Grafton House in Little Darkgate Street, near the entrance to the castle grounds, where another professor, George A Schott, lived with his wife. It was reported that '...Dr Schott at once appeared at the window and, appearing to be greatly annoyed, declared that he was British born, being a native of Yorkshire.' However, the crowd accused him or his wife of playing the German nationalistic song 'The Watch on the Rhine' on the piano every evening. He denied this but '...the crowd was in no humour to accept denial and asked him also to leave the town in twenty-four hours.'

Somewhat perversely, the British Nationality and Status of Aliens Act passed on 7 August 1914 stated that the wife of an alien, even if she were British-born, would be treated as an alien, while an alien wife of a British subject would be regarded as being British. Thus, according to the law, Mrs Ethé – born in Lichfield – was deemed to be German, while Mrs Schott – born in Germany – was considered British.

When some of the crowd returned to Schott's house the following day, it was to express its support for a perturbed Schott, who they now acknowledged was English. However, some wag commented, 'but made in Germany' and there was still some suspicion as to his loyalties. Indeed, had the mob been seriously seeking to root out potential German spies then they may have found the Schotts to be more likely candidates than the Ethés.

An eccentric and gregarious academic like Ethé, with an English wife whose brother had joined the British Army, was improbable spy material. However, although the 46-year-old Schott had been born in Bradford, his parents were both German and the language of the home was probably German. They called their son by his middle name, Adolphus or Adolph. Schott had an outstanding scientific mind, was fluent in three languages, and was an excellent chess player, a brilliant pianist and a capable golfer. His wife, Antonia Schweizer, whom he married in 1913, was German. They had been attending a wedding in Germany in August 1914 and had had to leave in a hurry when war broke out. Their friend, the groom, had been called up by the German Army soon after the wedding ceremony.

Schott was no doubt a more obvious prospect for any clandestine spying activities than Ethé, and because of their strong links with Germany, he and his wife could easily have been driven out of town with the Ethés. There is, of course, no evidence to suggest that the Schotts were spies or even pro-German during the war, but a degree of suspicion remained in the town. Following the sinking of the passenger liner the SS *Lusitania* by a German U-boat in May 1915, there were further anti-German demonstrations throughout the country and Schott received threatening letters. According to T Gwynn Jones, 'He was naturally much distressed & his wife was in terror'. Members of the College's staff stayed overnight at his home on three successive nights but there was no repeat of the events of October 1914. In April 1918 the Revd R J Rees received a letter from Schott reporting that Rees's two young boys had called Schott and his wife 'Huns'. Geraint and Goronwy (later Principal of the College) were reprimanded by their father and taken to see the Schotts to apologise.

*

Following the dramatic events of 15 October, the Ethés left town and the other Germans targeted by the mob, apart from the exonerated Schotts, were also soon gone. A demonstration held at the same location at the end of North Parade on the following day was on a much smaller scale but the language remained belligerent. Dr Harries, once more employing his talent for populist demagoguery, referred to 'German brutes' and the need to '...clear them out, but do not touch them for they are lousy and stink of German sausage. Put them in the sea to clean them and then send them off by train.' He and T J Samuel had received telegrams praising the townspeople. One from London read:

> Bravo Aberystwyth; but was there no street lamp and hempen rope available for the murderers?

Later, some of the mob elements visited premises in the town to check that the Germans had all left.

*

The nature and motives of the protesters over the two-day period of demonstrating are worth examining, even though we have few individual names save for the main speakers. Most of the crowd of roughly 2,000, representing about a quarter of the town's population, should not be considered necessarily belligerent in nature. The only photograph of some of the marchers on their way to Ethé's house was taken in Llanbadarn Road by a local photographer, Arthur Lewis. This was published in the *Western Mail* but the original has not survived and the printed copy is indistinct. The crowd appears to consist of flat-capped working men and some women, who all appeared to be respectably dressed. As suggested earlier, they were probably there to openly support family members in the armed services and would not necessarily have wished to physically harm Ethé or his compatriots. Indeed, this was the tenor of a letter by 'Ystwyth' to the *Western Mail* defending the protesters, of which he was one:

> ...there was no thought of attacking anyone... No one attempted to force his way into the house [Ethé's], or in any way made any attempt to use force.

As the protest was held on a Wednesday, when shops closed at lunchtime, we can presume that the crowd was boosted by a number of shopkeepers and their employees. Some children left school for the afternoon, as was recorded in the Aberystwyth Council School log book for that day:

> Several boys were absent this afternoon following a procession of townspeople who protested against the presence in the town of some Germans.

To these pupils, the protest was no doubt a source of much fun. They had in any case been indoctrinated in their classes about the glories of the British Empire, as arrangements were well in hand to celebrate Trafalgar Day on 21 October.

There were clearly mob elements leading the crowd. We have only one name, Bill Morgan, who probably carried the red ensign and was involved in the altercations in Caradog Road and elsewhere. He was 49 years old and is described as a 'boatman' in the 1911 census and his wife, Elizabeth, as a 'fish dealer'. He had lived in some of the more impoverished areas in the town and in 1911 was living in Portland Road, not one of the town's most salubrious streets at that time. As a boatman, Morgan had no doubt gathered together several protesters from among his acquaintances in the harbour area of the town, some of whom were likely to have friends or family members in the Navy or on merchant ships.

Bill Morgan was no stranger to mobs. In August 1888 he had had been involved in an altercation in Terrace Road when PC Joseph had tried to arrest an inebriated local. A mob tried to prevent this, and during the fracas it was alleged that Bill Morgan kicked the constable in the back. He then tried to hide among the crowd but was identified by witnesses as the culprit. At the magistrates' court he was found guilty of assault and given a fine of £5, which he could not pay. The alternative was a month's imprisonment with hard labour, which he served at Swansea Prison. The prison records note that he was 5 feet

7½ inches tall with brown hair and that he claimed to be a Baptist. We know no more about him but he appears to have been somewhat of a ruffian, or at least hot-tempered, and some of those responsible for the most unruly behaviour among the crowd were most likely of a similar disposition.

Whereas many of the demonstrators were probably chapel members, the ministers and deacons were not involved. On that day the Minister of Seilo, the Revd T E Roberts, together with some other prominent Methodists from the town, was in Ysbyty Ystwyth to unveil a memorial to the revivalist Dafydd Morgan. Clearly neither T E Roberts nor the Minister of Tabernacl Chapel, the Revd R J Rees, had prior knowledge of the demonstration. Rees noted in his diary for that day that he had '...heard great hubbub towards Promenade & on enquiry hear workmen are in commotion because of Dr Ethé's return last night and supposed official recognition of him by authorities. Mass meeting at Shiloh at 1.'

This suggests that the events of October had little to do with narrow Nonconformity, as has been suggested by some. The identifiable leading figures who expressed anti-German feelings during this period were mostly incomers into the town. T J Samuel was Aberystwyth-born, but Enoch Davies (Ruthin), Dr Harries (Fishguard), James Matson (Kent), Frank Bramhall Haigh (Lancashire), Edward Llewellin (Abergavenny), Charles Pancheon (Norfolk) and Tom Rowlands (Cardigan) were all born elsewhere. Although Harries and Rowlands had lived in the town for most of their lives, these incomers brought with them a different perspective. Matson and Llewellin were both hoteliers; Harries, Pancheon and probably Rowlands were churchmen; Harries, Llewelin and Rowlands were Conservatives. Haigh's views were particularly virulent, questioning the loyalties of a Warsaw-born hairdresser called Adler, despite his presenting valid naturalisation documents. Haigh suggested that the matter of naturalisation should be looked into to see if any naturalised aliens were in touch with the enemy. Matson noted that it should not be forgotten that there were female aliens as well as male aliens, presumably suggesting that they might be spies.

This is not to apportion the blame to outsiders alone. The majority of the protesters were from Aberystwyth itself, but it was the growing secularisation of the town and external influences, such as the expanding readership of English newspapers, which accounted for the endemic jingoism and anti-German feeling. Ultimately Ethé was driven from the town because he was a German rather than for any other reason.

*

The affair did not end with the ejection from the town of all Germans, as the town council and the College authorities remained at loggerheads over the treatment of Ethé. The majority of the councillors expected the College to dismiss Ethé but, though absent, he remained in post until 1915, when it was decided that he should retire on a small pension. To their credit, the College authorities held firm on the issue, despite complaints from several councillors, such as Dr Harries, who accused the College governors of being '...biased and prejudiced in granting a pension to a Hun.' In retribution, the town council refused to nominate a member to serve on the College's Court in 1916.

It has been suggested that Ethé affair was used by the town council as a means to attack the College. Indeed the student magazine *The Dragon* suggested as much in its May 1916 edition, claiming that the Ethé case was '...a disingenuous expression of a deep-rooted enmity to this college.' To Principal T F Roberts, 'it was not the hooligans; it was the responsible leaders of the town who did this.' However, although relations had become soured, there is no reason to suppose that there was any degree of conspiracy. To some of the town councillors, the College's crime was to remain loyal to an alien enemy and to afford him special treatment. There have always been tensions between 'town and gown', but these came to the fore over this issue during challenging wartime circumstances.

*

Of the main characters in this dramatic story, Enoch Davies, benefited least. Later in 1914, he was heavily defeated in the Aberystwyth municipal elections for Ward 3 while Dr Harries headed the poll in Ward 2. T J Samuel had already been elected an alderman and in 1920 was awarded the MBE for his services as Chair of the Aberystwyth Association of the National War Savings Movement.

In the College, Principal T F Roberts died in August 1919 and was succeeded in the post by the Registrar, J H Davies, who had remained in contact with Professor Ethé. Professor Schott later became Vice-Principal of the College but four years after retirement in 1933, he died suddenly. Professor Ethé, having been in his own words '...hunted... down like a wild beast', found employment with the India Office and the British Museum but died in Clifton, Bristol in June 1917. As the College's historian, E L Ellis, stated incisively, '...he was a casualty of war just as certainly as any young soldier killed at the Front.'

Hermann Ethé (1844 — 1917)

Yn y lle hwn ymgasglodd torf niferus o drigolion Aberystwyth yn Hydref 1914 i alltudio'r Athro Hermann Ethé o'r dref oherwydd ei genedligrwydd Almaenig. Gadawodd Ethé drannoeth, ac ni ddychwelodd i'w gartref yn Ffordd Caradog nac i'w swydd ym Mhrifysgol Aberystwyth. Bu farw ym Mryste ym 1917. Gosodir y gofeb hon gan Gyngor Tref Aberystwyth yn y gobaith na phrofa neb erledigaeth debyg yn ein tref fyth eto.

A large mob of Aberystwyth inhabitants gathered here in October 1914 to drive Professor Hermann Ethé from the town because of his German nationality. Ethé left the following day, never to return to his home in Caradog Road or to his work at Aberystwyth University. He died in Bristol in 1917. This plaque is placed by Aberystwyth Town Council in the hope that nobody will experience such persecution in our town again.

Hier versammelten sich im Oktober 1914 Einwohner von Aberystwyth mit der Absicht, Professor Hermann Ethé gewaltsam aus der Stadt zu vertreiben, weil er Deutscher war. Ethé verliess Aberystwyth am nächsten Morgen, um nie wieder in sein Haus in Caradog Road oder an die Universität von Aberystwyth zurückzukehren. Er verstarb 1917 in Bristol. Diese Gedenktafel wurde vom Stadtrat von Aberystwyth in der Hoffnung errichtet, dass niemandem in unserer Stadt jemals wieder ein solches Unrecht geschieht.

Plaque near the Morlan Centre in Aberystwyth
(author's own photograph)

Two Christian Intellectuals: R J Rees and T Gwynn Jones

A day of nerves, of anxiety – the fear, the burden,
the horror of war upon me and great questionings
as to rightness of my country's cause.

R J REES'S DIARY, 4 AUGUST 1914

I am at Ystrad Meurig... It is quiet and restful here, and I find it
impossible to realize that possibly the greatest crime in the history
of the world is being perpetrated not very far away.

T GWYNN JONES'S JOURNAL, AUGUST 1914

DURING THE EVENING service led by the Reverend R J Rees at Tabernacl Chapel, Aberystwyth on 17 October 1915, the prominent poet and academic T Gwynn Jones arose from his pew and led his family out of the chapel, avowedly in protest at the Minister's prayer for victory in the war. This dramatic event has remained one of the most referred-to occurrences in the history of the town during the war (although it has been incorrectly told by some historians). More importantly, it reflects different streams of thought and action represented by two of the most gifted and perceptive residents of the town during that period.

Both protagonists in this incident, R J Rees and T Gwynn Jones, kept diaries which survive, written mainly in English despite their use of Welsh in their professional activities. The diaries were also quite different in nature. Rees wrote faithfully in note form almost every day about his activities and financial transactions. He included the names of people he had met but seldom provided any great detail on the content of his conversations and only occasionally commented on his personal perspective on events. T Gwynn Jones's one-volume diary is more of a journal written on an occasional basis, but replete with anecdotes and telling observations on people and incidents.

Before the war, R J Rees and T Gwynn Jones were relatively close friends. According to Rees's diary for September 1912, the two of them went for 'a brief walk and chat' on one occasion and on another evening that month, Jones and his wife had 'supper & chat' at Rees's house in North Road. Although we have no record of their conversations, it is likely that they spoke mostly of Christian faith, theology, philosophy and literature.

In July of that year, Jones sent Rees a poem which was related in some way to a sermon or sermons given by Rees. The poem does not seem to have survived, unless it is an early version of 'Lux Mundi', a poem published in the Welsh Methodist journal, *Y Drysorfa*, in 1914. Rees's letter of thanks illuminates the depth of their relationship:

> ...it is a great privilege that I have such as you to listen to me and that the common worship moves the depths of your life. But I have a secret to tell you. Whilst you reveal the depths of your griefs and hopes – now dead you say – the depths of your possession for the True and Right in a world of Falsehood and Cunning – I dream of something else for you. I dream of the heights you can yet stand on and sing. Our Age needs a great poet of Faith. You have been fostered under Faith's wing. For years you have trod the dark places and found Faith's realities illusions – and yet I believe other

Revd R J Rees
(courtesy of The National
Library of Wales)

T Gwynn Jones

realities of Faith are forming within you. It is the very intensity and glory of your ideal which makes this world so garish to you and yet One Day I am hoping – after all the struggle and stress – Sturm und Drang ['storm and stress'] – that Ideal will descend like Our Lord into the Flesh, and life's distractions and defeats to serve this age of ours to find beyond the first Youth of Innocence the Eternal Youth of the Child of God. And I dream at times that Epic of Faith will be sung by you – not in terms of the creeds and not for the sake of the churches, but for the Lord of your life and mine. I'm coming up one night next week. We'll get out for a while on the hill tops. Ever yours in the ties of friendship.

Jones's opinion of Rees was equally respectful. In June 1913 he wrote of him to his old friend E Morgan Humphreys:

I am very, very friendly with him – he is a gentleman with whom you can talk, and become intimate. [translation]

Despite these 'ties of friendship' and intimacy, their reactions to war in 1914 and subsequently were quite different and represent a divergence of opinion which is worth examining.

*

Richard Jenkin Rees was born at Riwel Isaf, a farm on the outskirts of Bow Street, four miles north of Aberystwyth, in September 1868. However, when he was still a small child, his family removed to London, later running a small dairy business in Stepney Green in the East End. They were devout members of Jewin, the most prominent Welsh Methodist chapel in London, where Rees's father, John Rees, became a deacon.

Following a wide-ranging education at the City of London School, Rees returned to his native county to study at Aberystwyth College, gaining a degree in Classics in 1889. He planned to study medicine but failed to pass the entrance exam and, during a turbulent period in his life, he became convinced that he was being called by God to enter the ministry. He attended the school of theology at Mansfield College, Oxford, graduating with a first-class honours degree in 1892 and becoming a minister of Calvinistic Methodist chapels in Pwllheli and subsequently in Cardiff.

As a young minister, he was described as being 'bright, vigilant and energetic' and gained a reputation as a powerful preacher in the tradition of the giants of the pulpit of previous generations. He was a Calvinist, believing that he was one of God's elect, but he also had a social conscience. He once said that pastors '...had to deal with communities as physicians had to deal with patients. They were the general practitioners of the spiritual.' He was also an uncompromising advocate of temperance.

His youngest son, Goronwy, later a controversial Principal at Aberystwyth College, wrote vividly about his father:

> When I saw my father in the pulpit, I hardly distinguished between him and the God whose religion he preached.

In 1902, Rees was attracted to what would have been at that time the coveted position of Minister of Tabernacl Chapel in Aberystwyth, the equivalent perhaps of being appointed a bishop or cardinal in other churches. The following year he, his wife Apphia and their young family moved to Aberystwyth to live in a three-storey manse called Rhos (now Penygeulan) on North Road, overlooking the town.

Memorably described by one writer as a 'temple-fortress', Tabernacl Chapel was one of the largest chapels in Wales and boasted a substantial membership in excess of 700 adult communicants, together with a thriving Sunday School. The Minister was, by the nature of his office, highly influential in Methodist circles and in the social life of the town. Rees remained there for nearly twenty years, though far from entirely satisfied by the vicissitudes of his pastorate. He found himself in the midst of powerful local deacons whose disagreements and factionalism, both within and outside the chapel, were difficult to cope with. This was partly because his involvement with local and national affairs did not always sit easily with his pastoral duties. There are occasional comments in his diary to his state of mind; for example this from 5 January 1912:

> In state of mental unrest these days – Faith is hard pressed. Dissatisfaction grips one.

The previously mentioned issue of the selling of alcoholic drinks at Aberystwyth Golf Club in 1912 proved particularly contentious, with a clear split between those who championed a freedom of choice in the matter and others, including Rees, who were fundamentally intransigent in their temperance beliefs. One prominent deacon, Arthur Jones, a bank manager by profession, sought advice on whether he should resign from his chapel duties over the issue. Rees noted in his diary that Jones '...had been in a state of collapse and has retired out of action & is hiding behind others.'

'We sail through unquiet seas these days' was typical of comments made by Rees in his diaries. He was also to write in 1912, 'I feel discontented & changeable these days: burdened by the sense I am not in my proper sphere & wonder whether I am caged up or not away from my true sphere! The Lord give me his peace.'

He wrote on 9 September 1913 of his '...wrath & contempt on the spirit of suspicion & envy prevailing among God's people. Unwise & uncharitable doubtless my spirit & language.'

On his birthday on 10 September 1913, he wrote:

> 45 years old today – feel the battle itself harder every year – to keep one's heart pure, unselfish, zealous – a greater task than self can accomplish: Christ alone can and will do it. To him I commit myself, my ministry & my beloved ones.

He was conscientious and hard-working, as a diary entry from 11 January 1905 records:

A specimen day of a minister's life is offered me by today's work
– 1) a wedding of Rev W E Harris 2) funeral [Mrs Molyneaux] 3)
reading a will 4) visiting a sister who has fallen 5) visiting a family
where son in law only married a fortnight ago is seriously ill 6)
Bible class 7) Public mtg 8) officers mtg – background home life,
distant mountain range. God & his things.

His family life was not always easy and he complained that
his financial position was never comfortable. In 1915 he wrote
in his diary regarding a meeting of the College's finance sub-
committee on which he served: '...oh the farce of things – here
am I *heb feddu dim* [owning nothing] in virtue of appointment
on Committee able to sign cheques for hundreds.'

Rees's diary and his careful accounting show that his salary
was £200 a year, which, augmented by other activities, gave
him an income in 1912 of £451 16s. 9d. His expenditure was
a little over £428. He commented on 24 February 1912: 'I live
day by day.'

Before the war, Rees had conducted several services in
his chapel specifically for the local branch of the Territorial
Army and had also expressed his views on the military at a
South Wales Calvinistic Methodist Association meeting held
in March 1912:

It was with very great difficulty that the territorials' organisation
had placed itself in keeping with Welsh national sentiment. There
was a love of peace in Wales. The trade of a soldier had not always
been a trade that even they, as Nonconformists, had been in favour
of. Many of them today, in the responsibility of their citizenship,
had been prepared to support the formation of a land army of this
kind for the defence of their own shores...

He was clearly not, then, averse to the military in the years
before the war, and from there it was but a short step to
supporting Britain's involvement in the war in August 1914.

*

T Gwynn Jones was, like Rees, the son of a farmer and from Methodist stock. He was born on 10 October 1871 at Bettws yn Rhos, Denbighire. Unlike R J Rees, however, he was very much self-taught and did not receive a university education. He made up for this by reading voraciously and honing his skills as a writer during a long period as a journalist. He became celebrated as a poet when he won the chair at the 1902 National Eisteddfod for his *awdl 'Ymadawiad Arthur'*, and was regarded as a pioneer in the development of modern Welsh poetry.

Jones came to Aberystwyth in 1909 to work as a cataloguer at the National Library of Wales, where he was able to expand his already prodigious knowledge of Welsh literature. He was, however, uncomfortable with the anglicising influence on the Library of its formidable first Librarian, John Ballinger, whom he once described as an autocrat. In 1913 Jones was appointed a lecturer in Welsh at Aberystwyth College; a role which better suited his talents.

During this period, he lived in a house called Eirlys on the Buarth, less than half a mile from R J Rees's home on North Road. He had not been a regular attender of chapels for some time but he was a member of Tabernacl Chapel in 1910, although he seems to have given up his membership subsequently. While his wife remained a member, Jones had become a *gwrandawr*, literally a 'listener' – an 'adherent' who attended the chapel but was not a member. Unlike Rees, he could not be certain that he was one of God's elect.

Jones was critical of the churches in general during this period, having suggested in 1909 in the regular column he wrote for *The North Wales Times* that:

> The pulpit tends to become the mouthpiece of militarism and other barbarities, and the [political] platform the place for the exposition of modern Christianity.

He was also critical of what he termed 'cheap patriotism'. In January 1914 he spoke at a dinner in London hosted by David

Lloyd George, at that time the Chancellor of the Exchequer, condemning 'professional patriotism'.

*

In early August 1914, during the days prior to Britain entering a war which had already begun on the continent, both Jones and Rees were dismayed by fast-moving events. In his diary for 1 August, Rees expressed his horror of war: 'We are on the verge of a great disaster...'

On the same day, Jones composed a Welsh poem entitled 'Rhyfel' ['War'], which would be published in the Welsh-language newspaper *Y Faner* on 8 August. In the caustic mode which he sometimes favoured over the romantic form for which he is most famous as a poet, he berated warmongers and their hypocrisy. To him 'the killer with crimson hands' is war's 'magnificent god'.

> *Ymaith a'ch ffug wareiddiad,*
> *A'ch ffôl dosturi i gyd,*
> *Gonest addolwch y lleiddiad*
> *Sy fyth yn rheoli'ch byd:*
> *Dilynwch eich bwystfil deidiau,*
> *Sernwch Y Crist tan draed,*
> *Rhuthrwch i'r gad yn heidiau,*
> *Ymdreiglwch ym meddwdod gwaed!*

> [Away with your fake civilisation,
> And all your foolish compassion,
> Honestly worship the killer
> Who forever controls your world:
> Follow your beastly forefathers,
> Trample the Christ underfoot,
> Rush to battle in swarms,
> Wallow in drunken blood!]

*

Two days later, 3 August, Jones visited Rees in North Road, staying until late that evening discussing the prospect of war. Rees makes no further comment in his diary but Jones refers to the visit:

> I went to see a ministerial friend, for whom I had some respect, with the object of suggesting that a meeting be called in the town to join the protest against participating in the struggle. He expressed his sympathy with the suggestion, but was afraid that at that time of the year, when there were many visitors in the town, people would be too busy to attend. He admitted that he would have been delighted if on a previous Sunday, I had moved an anti-war resolution during one of the services. I explained to him that my only reason for not having done so was that I was not a church member. He replied that he thought I was nearer the Christian standpoint than most people who were members.

The following day Rees noted in his diary:

> A day of nerves, of anxiety – the fear, the burden, the horror of war upon me and great questionings as to rightness of my country's cause: Gt [great?] speech last night by Sir Ed.[ward] Grey [the Foreign Secretary], a practical declaration of war with Germany. All I meet nearly anti-Germans but I more pro than otherwise & yet cannot but feel their policy is one of war than otherwise.

Jones meanwhile met with two unnamed church members, to whom he refers as 'A' and 'B':

> Both agreed with me that war was a horrible thing, but they said we had no option, apparently. I appealed to their Christian professions. B said that Christ was not against war, & cited his words to the effect that He had not come to bring peace but a sword on earth, & his command on another occasion to someone to procure a sword. I suggested that exponents disagreed as to the meaning of these passages, but that there could be no doubt as to the injunction to turn the other cheek. This he admitted, and when I gave it as my belief the non-resisting nation would have

been the strongest on earth, he said I ought to have been a church member, & that one man with such a belief would have done more for Christianity than all the priests. The same person, within a very short time stated publicly that he considered it a religious duty to fight "in this war", & that he was ashamed of his country because the recruits were not more numerous. My friend the minister [R J Rees] also practically adopted the same view, & within a month appeared as a speaker on recruiting platforms.

That night, war was declared and the following day Rees wrote: 'In war fever all day'. He also received a letter from his brother, Morgan, a medical inspector with the Local Government Board in London, who commented:

> The War, of which I have spoken to you on many an occasion, has come at length. Our country could not keep out without losing her good name. But the cost for a time will be great.

Clearly this had become Rees's view also.

Meanwhile, on 6 August, Jones was busy writing an essay for the Welsh journal *Y Traethodydd* entitled *'Trechaf treisied'* ['Let he that is strongest violate'], in which he attacked militarism and the disregard for Christ's teachings:

> There has never been a more massive crime against it than is occurring between the 'Christian' countries of Europe today. [translation]

He claimed that even if Germany was to be defeated, the same would be the result – 'a Victory for Militarism.'

He concluded:

> It is the animal element in our nature which it is our duty to conquer. Once more in the history of Europe, the animal has won supremacy... Christians have lost one other opportunity, because they still did not understand the principle which they profess. It puts humanity's ability and knowledge to the service of its animal paw. We are all in this transgression. [translation]

He also wrote to an old friend, E Morgan Humphreys, on the same day:

> I have no appetite for anything... The devil has gone to heaven, and the world is going to hell, and we claim to be Christians. [translation]

*

Both Rees and Jones went on holiday during the following week, though they did not travel too far from Aberystwyth. Rees and his family took a cottage near the village of Ystumtuen, while less than eight miles away, as a crow might have flown across the sprawling hills of Ceredigion, Jones took a family break at Pen y Graig in Ystrad Meurig. The distance in miles might have been small but the distance in viewpoints was widening inexorably.

Rees was '...glad to be away – war fever & rumours & conversations taking over whole time.' He did not take his diary with him and there are no entries until the end of the month, by which time he had returned to Aberystwyth, where he mentions 'war rumours of reverse damping all our spirits'.

Jones was more expansive in his journal:

> I am at Ystrad Meurig... It is quiet and restful here, and I find it impossible to realize that possibly the greatest crime in the history of the world is being perpetrated not very far away... It is in the afternoon, & I have been walking on the mountain. The world seemed very beautiful. Growth – fecundity – everywhere. On the mountain there were fern & gorse in which you could lose yourself; sheep & cattle peacefully grazing; rabbits playing about. Nothing seemed extraordinary & yet everything was wonderful. If I could always live here, I would do so, and be only interested in trees, flowers, animals, clouds, mists & such things. In time, I think I could forget everything else. I shall certainly never see anything half so beautiful as those mountain-ash trees with their immense crop of berries, or anything half so free as that little girl

who went up the mountain as I was coming down, & stood singing on the topmost ridge.

This idyllic scene was disturbed by a passing stranger, a reservist on his way to war via the nearest railway station. Jones walks with him and discovers that he is going to "fight for his country". Jones imagines that he might be shot by '…a man very much like him, but whom he cannot see, & to whom he has certainly done no wrong… He was simply a thing to be shot down, by another such a thing, at the bidding & for the benefit of the social parasites who have always made, who still make, & who ever will make all wars.'

*

Any doubts which may have arisen in Rees's mind prior to the declaration of war had clearly disappeared by the end of August. On 2 September he, among many other dutiful citizens, was sworn in as a Special Constable at a meeting in the Drill Hall, Aberystwyth. He spoke with his usual vigour, but in a bellicose manner which reflected his commitment to the war effort. The local press included a full report:

> The Rev. R. J. Rees said he considered it a privilege to serve his King and country in any capacity. (Cheers). They were now going through a crisis – a vital crisis in the history of their fatherland – when their best men endured a searching of heart; when the question inevitably arose "What can I do for my country to safeguard its interest and existence?" Many of them had become too old to go into the firing line: and at that painful moment a good angel in the form of the Chief Constable appeared to show how some of them could take the first step and show by whole hearted steadfastness and fidelity the further line of duty for some of their younger brothers to consecrate themselves to more active service. (Cheers). In a town like Aberystwyth, devoid as it was of industries, the percentage of active manhood was small; but he saw yet a large number of young men about the streets who were

promising material for Lord Kitchener's army. (Great cheering). He had been a pro-German – an admirer of the genius of that great nation in its literature, poetry, art, and theology but he certainly was not an admirer of the spirit of brute force which animated its ruling classes in their treatment of small nationalities. (Cheers). That was a phase of German character that should appeal with irresistible force to Wales to stand unitedly and steadfastly in assisting to thwart so ignoble an ambition in an otherwise great power. (Cheers). The crisis was one in which even a small force might be sufficient to turn the balance of victory. (Cheers). Their forefathers – the long bowmen of Wales – turned the scale at Crecy. (Cheers). Picton, a distinguished Welshman, rendered signal service at Waterloo. (Cheers). Though a confirmed advocate of peace, he would be delighted to see a squad of young men from Aberystwyth deciding to sacrifice themselves on the altar of duty and patriotism for their country, for their homes, and for humanity. (Cheers).

During the following months, Rees appeared on many recruiting platforms throughout the county. In November 1914 he considered becoming an Army chaplain but decided against this because of 'home demands' and because soldiers were to be billeted in the town, and he considered 'his duty lies at home.' Indeed, he took the church parade at Tabernacl Chapel in December with 250 soldiers present.

*

Throughout the war, Jones continued to protest, notably through his poetry. His poem 'Pro Patria', composed in 1915, is fiercely uncompromising on the inhumanity of war while his lengthy ode 'Madog' referred to his belief that patriotism was devilish in nature. He claimed too that he was a 'pacifist with the emphasis on the fist'.

Meanwhile Rees noted his 'flagging spiritual enthusiasm' but three days later, on 27 January 1915, wrote:

Midnight Friday I had a sense of the Divine Presence giving me perfect peace – one of those rare experiences God has given me from time to time at some intervals.

He continued to see Jones on several occasions but, according to Rees, Jones remained intransigent in his views.

Their disagreement came to a head on 17 October 1915. Rees's description of the incident is brief:

Tabernacl – preached twice with ordinary results – no great success but yet intense: After prayer in evening service T.G.J. left service – for what reason I cannot surmise unless for some cause of protest on his part!

Jones, however, was more forthcoming:

One evening when the Rev R J Rees officiated, I failed to put up with it any longer, & left the building when they were singing after the introductory prayer, which was no better than a barbarian's appeal to the god of his tribe, which god was thanked for the willingness of his creatures to serve their country & beseeched to grant victory to his fighting hosts – not even a suggestion that he should decide the justice of the quarrel for himself.

Soon after he was to write to a friend stating that he had finished with Nonconformity for ever.

Apart from the inevitable gossip which circulated in the town, Jones's protest had little effect. Another poet and friend of Jones, Dewi Morgan, did resign his membership of Tabernacl Chapel during the ensuing months but Rees and the chapel continued as before.

Jones's anti-war stance strengthened. He wrote to a friend:

Almost everything is depressing me, these devilish days, and I cannot do anything with any energy, except to oppose war and warmongers. I have almost finished with 'patriotism' – the last refuge of the scoundrel, as Johnson once said.

Perhaps surprisingly, in the light of his feelings about Tabernacl Chapel and Nonconformism in general, the war intensified Jones's religious beliefs. During a discussion with Tegla Davies, a prominent Wesleyan minister who had suggested that the war had caused many to become atheists, Jones replied that it had made him a Christian. He stated that '...he had believed that the human race had developed slowly and surely through education and civilizing influences into something nebulous which we call God's Dominion. Today I see that there are only two choices – commit suicide, as we are doing, or regeneration through our Lord Jesus Christ.'

Jones's journal included many second-hand anecdotes on military incompetence, on the cruelty shown to German prisoners, on the extent of venereal disease among the soldiers, and most tellingly on the attitudes of his fellow Welshmen. The famous educationalist and recruiter Sir O M Edwards, for example, in his opinion had by 1917 '...a hunted harassed look about him'.

The journal also contains references to Rees's activities, such as in the case of the conscientious objector D J Davies (see Chapter VIII). Jones noted that Rees (though not named, we can be sure it was he) had stated that he would fight to the end to oppose compulsion but when conscription was implemented in the spring of 1916, he had not raised his voice against it and had privately condemned conscientious objection.

*

Though Jones could not be accused of living in an 'ivory tower', he was not directly affected by the tragedy of war. He may well have known some of the students who were killed but he lost no close relatives. Rees's experiences were much closer to the action. In September 1915 he comforted the family of a chapel member, David Felix, one of the 14 members of Tabernacl Chapel who lost their lives in the war. Their families expected their minister to support them in their grief and Rees was not found wanting.

In July 1916, Rees went to London to see his brother, Morgan, who was off to France as a captain with the Royal Army Medical Corps, 'on the great adventure'. In late October he was given special permission to cross to France to see Morgan, who had been severely wounded at Thiepval. By the time he had reached the hospital in Boulogne, Morgan had '...passed away to God's eternal rest'. Rees saw his brother's body, with his leg amputated, in the mortuary and conducted the funeral at Boulogne Eastern Cemetery on the last day of October.

In his diary he wrote of his 'beautiful, unselfish brother':

Morgan's departure more & more heavily presses on us – *mae hiraeth llawn fy nghalon ac eto gorfoddelaf yn ei aberth a'i ysbryd tra rhagorol – llwfr ydwyf o'i cydmaru ag ef.*

['my heart is full of yearning and yet I rejoice in his sacrifice and his superb spirit – I am cowardly in comparison with him.']

In 1917 the Ministry of National Service commissioned Rees to travel the length and breadth of the county to encourage men and women to assist the war effort by volunteering to undertake work under the National Service scheme. Over a four-week period in the spring, he addressed over 40 meetings. His speech at one meeting in Pontrhydfendigaid on 14 April 1917 was reported by the press in some detail:

His business that evening was to try and infuse enthusiasm into the people to undertake their duty to assist the Allies in bringing this terrible war to a speedy end. National service meant that all should be patriots not only in love for their country but also in serving it, defend[ing] it, and help[ing] it in the hour of peril and need. To do that effectively they should submit to some central authority, obey the call for help, and perform it with a will whatever sacrifices it entailed. They should remember the sacrifices made by our brave lads under great disadvantages as compared with the perfectly-equipped German armies. Our boys demurred not, grumbled not, but calmly struggled on as soldiers always did. "Their's [sic] not to reason why, their's [sic] but to do and die." No choice of work, no place to suit their fancy, or power to defer its performance at pleasure, but all had to stand at "attention" and be ready to set off on their task at the word of command. He was sure no one present considered themselves less brave or greater cowards than those at the front. None of them wished to be dubbed as cowards, and be regarded as the refuse of the community when the war was over because they now refused to do their part for their country and help those at the front. All they had to do was to enrol for national service and be ready to undertake work selected for them by those in control. The controller knew where help was most needed on farms, in mines, in munition works, in lumbering, and the hundreds of industries which provided for the needs of the army in all its varied work and for the nation. He hoped every one would say, *Wele fi, anfon fi* ['Here I am, send me'].

It was reported that '...the address was listened to with rapt attention and greatly appreciated.'

Clearly, there was little which Rees would not do for the war effort.

*

Among those who were called up near the end of the war was T Gwynn Jones. He was 47 years old and possessed a letter from the TB specialist of the county stating that he was suffering from tuberculosis and was therefore medically unfit for war service. However, probably as a means of victimisation, he was forced to attend a medical board at Lampeter on 3 July 1918, where he was examined by, as he wrote to a friend, *'meddygon y cigyddion'* ['the butchers' doctors'], and adjudged unfit for service. On his return that evening, Rees called on him and, despite his stance on recruitment, would no doubt have expressed his sympathy. Indeed, any animosity which might have soured their relationship is not evident. Any wounds were soon healed and after the war Jones became a member of Tabernacl Chapel once more.

In September 1919, Jones wrote an article on Rees for *Y Cymro* newspaper when the latter was appointed President of the South Wales Methodist Association. It is replete with fulsome praise of the minister as a preacher and as a shepherd of his flock. He describes in detail his preaching style, praising his ability to 'awaken the spirit and mind in man'. He notes Rees's talent for comforting and pacifying in the face of the hurt and disquiet brought about by storms and upheavals. He does not refer to their disputes but rather emphasises his friendship with Rees whom he describes as being 'gentle, generous and very supportive'.

*

It is difficult to appreciate how two friends, both imbued with Christian beliefs, could possess such divergent and entrenched views on such an enormous issue as the conduct of war, but both were men of principle and they retained their self-respect and the respect of others. In a message in Welsh to Jones written in March 1918, Rees wrote that he hoped they might walk in the Light – and that *Lux Mundi* would be for the two of them personally the light that would chase away the darkness.

V

Unpatriotic Farmers?

*Cardiganshire farmers have the reputation of being very
hospitable to strangers but very mean to those in their employ.
It would appear as if their naturally generous disposition has
been modified by the necessity of winning a modest livelihood
out of a particularly unkindly soil.*

EDGAR CHAPPELL, *WAGES AND CONDITIONS OF EMPLOYMENT IN
AGRICULTURE IN WALES*, 1918, CMD.24, VOL.1

*He was sorry to hear it said in a certain town lately that the
reason why the war was not ended was that the 'Godly' farmers
of Cardiganshire were praying for it to continue.*

MORGAN MORGAN AT A NATIONAL SERVICE MEETING AT CARDIGAN
CARDIGAN AND TIVY-SIDE ADVERTISER, 9 MARCH 1917

A 'DITTY' LAMPOONING the attitudes of farmers to the war
was published by several Welsh newspapers in January 1916.
Although it did not refer specifically to farmers in Ceredigion,
there is no doubt that it would have struck a chord with the
many critics of the farming community in the county.

The Unpatriotic Farmer's Ditty

I thank thee, Lord, for giving
Me a farm,
To keep me from recruiting

And alarm;
My eldest son's a foreman,
My second is a cowman,
My third is now a ploughman,
On the farm,
And ev'ry one's a "Star Man"
On the farm.

Let come recruiting sergeant
To the farm,
And take away the servant
From the farm.
My sons shall live in plenty,
High prices make me wealthy,
And I shall live quite happy
On the farm,
And sing to War a ditty
On the farm.

Let warriors die a-fighting
For the right;
We farmers are enjoying,
Sitting tight;
Our sons are home together
Far, far from serious danger
And I grow fat and prosper
Sitting tight,
While others join and muster for the fight.

The main complaints about farmers, as related in the ditty, were associated with accusations of profiteering from the war as a consequence of the increase in prices for agricultural produce and also the alleged tendency of farmers to protect their sons and their most expert farmhands from enlistment, while ordinary agricultural labourers were being recruited. The latter complaint was exacerbated following conscription and the formation in 1916 of Military Service Tribunals, which were dominated by farmers in rural counties such as

Ceredigion (for the activities of the Tribunals, see Chapter VI). This essay discusses the grounds for some of the allegations against the farmers.

*

The nature of rural society was changing during the early years of the twentieth century. The great landed estates were in decline and the hold of the gentry on agricultural communities was waning, although the widespread sale of lands by the Ceredigion gentry was more evident after the war. The social structure was also changing in other ways, particularly as a result of the mechanisation of farming practices. The lowest strata of agricultural society in Ceredigion – the cottagers who had no significant land to farm, and the agricultural labourers – suffered most from these developments. The cottagers had relied on providing their labour to farmers at times of hay and corn harvest, in return for strips of land to grow potatoes. However, this mutual obligation was breaking down and, as a consequence of mechanisation, the need for large crews of labourers was becoming increasingly unnecessary. At the same time, in the decades before the war, many farm labourers had left the countryside to work in the collieries of south Wales – some on a temporary basis, while others settled there permanently.

Some of the richer tenant farmers were able to buy their holdings or consolidate them, and the more substantial farmers, both freeholders and tenants, became increasingly prominent in public affairs. More often than not, they were chapel deacons whose influence was apparent in community activities. They flexed their political muscles in county council elections, with many of the councillors in rural Ceredigion being farmers, standing under the banner of the Liberal Party. They were sometime referred to as 'Radicals', harking back to the great battles of the nineteenth century over tithes and tenancies, but they became increasingly conservative in outlook and tended to represent the interests of the larger farmers.

Farmers were also involved with the National Farmers' Union, formed in 1908, with the majority of members coming from the north of the county. They also sat on public bodies, such as the Cardiganshire War Agricultural Committee (CWAC) formed in the autumn of 1915. It was only the more prosperous farmers, usually those who farmed over 100 acres (about 12% of the total holdings for the county), who could be active in this way, as they were able to employ sufficient farmhands to allow them time to undertake public duties.

When war was declared, farmers became subject to the regulations of the Defence of the Realm Act (known as DORA), which was passed by Parliament at the outset of the war, giving the Government wide-ranging powers. It was subsequently amended to cover a myriad of offences. It was forbidden, for example, to feed chickens or horses with bread because it was considered to be wasteful. The lighting of bonfires was banned, as they might alert the enemy. A well-known farmer from the north of the county, J M Jenkins of Cerrigcaranau, was fined five shillings by the Tal-y-bont Petty Sessions Court in February 1917 for permitting '...Cerrigcaranau uchaf bog to be on fire at 7 p.m. which showed a light at sea contrary to DORA.'

*

Before the war, Britain had relied on imports for 60% of its food supply but, as these became more limited by the constraints of wartime, there was pressure to grow more crops. This was problematic for farmers in Ceredigion, where much of the land was more suited to grass production and stock rearing. Arable farming acreage had been in decline in the county for a number of years and, in general, only a small proportion of cultivated land in Wales was devoted to grain.

The county committees set up by the Board of Agriculture, in association with the county councils, were a direct response to fears of food shortages. They had no statutory powers but were rather 'voluntary associations for a national purpose in a time of crisis.' They encouraged farmers to grow more crops but could not use compulsion or offer inducements, which limited their effectiveness. These county committees were supported by local committees which were able to give assistance and advice to farmers, smallholders and labourers. They would also report to the county committees, which would then compile progress reports and make recommendations to the Board of Agriculture.

The county committees tended to be dominated by farmers and county councillors. The first chair of CWAC was Councillor John Jones JP of Cwmere, a substantial freehold farm on the road between Felinfach and Temple Bar in the Aeron Valley. He was a pillar of the local community, including the local Independent chapel Ty'ngwndwn, which stood adjacent to his land. He had published a number of studies on farming and forestry and, apart from being a Liberal county councillor, he also served as a governor of Aberaeron County School and was a member of the Welsh Agricultural Council. In 1916 he was appointed Chair of the county's Military Service Tribunal (see Chapter VI). He and his family were, according to local sources, deemed to be a notch above the ordinary farmer at that time.

Other members of CWAC included Thomas Davies JP, a farmer and county councillor from Bronwion, Bettws Ifan, Alderman J Walter Davies, Forest Hall, Llangybi, and Councillor Daniel Jenkin Williams, Argoed Hall, Tregaron. These farmers were supported on CWAC by officers such as D J Morgan, the County Agricultural Officer and, most notably, by the Agricultural Commissioner for Wales, Professor (later Sir) Bryner Jones, the pre-eminent expert on agriculture in Wales, who was based at the College in Aberystwyth. Another expert who attended some of the meetings was George Stapledon, advisory Botanist at the College who, in a number of meetings held across the county in 1915, emphasised the importance of improving the fertility of the soil and the selection of appropriate seeds. In 1917 Stapledon was called to London to join the new Department for Food Production and later became the first director of The Welsh Plant Breeding Station near Aberystwyth.

In their initial meetings, CWAC considered various recommendations made by sub-committees, the first of which was in favour of establishing small co-operative implement societies for the purchase, or hire, of labour-saving machinery such as muck spreaders, potato diggers, disc harrows and seeders. The recommendation was adopted, as well as other recommendations in favour of increasing the yield and acreage of oats and of approaching the Loan Board with the view to helping societies and individuals to reclaim land. However, a suggestion in favour of bringing into cultivation common lands, especially in the vicinity of towns, was not adopted. It was agreed to support a recommendation to the Agricultural Council in favour of the registration of women and to arrange demonstrations of the working of motor ploughs and heavy disc harrows. It was also agreed to inform the Board of Agriculture of the prevalence of poultry disease and of husk in young cattle, which seemed to be on the increase.

There was increasing concern in the Government during 1916 regarding food supplies and following the formation of a new administration in December of that year, with Lloyd George as Prime Minister, it was decided to intervene directly in farming practice. Lloyd George's clarion call to farmers was unmistakeable:

> Every sack of food you raise is worth ammunition, is worth a
> gun, to use in this great struggle, and we ask you to come into the
> fighting line with your food.

It was recognised that local co-operation was required, and the County War Agriculture Committees were reformed into County War Agriculture Executive Committees which were given wide-ranging powers, notably to increase the amount of ploughed land and the growing of crops.

The Cardiganshire War Agriculture Executive Committee (CWAEC), established in early 1917, was once more dominated by farmers and county councillors. Councillor Richard Evans, Crynga-mawr, Blaenannerch, became Chairman and his service to agriculture was subsequently rewarded in 1918 with an MBE. Other members included E J Evans of Cnwc-y-barcud, Llangwyryfon and J Bunce Morgan of Glanfred, Llanfihangel Genau'r Glyn. Another John Jones also served on the committee; he farmed Penwern in Cilcennin and was also a county councillor.

Agents were employed to visit farms to ensure that sufficient farmland was being ploughed. Tractors and teams of horses were acquired to assist farmers in ploughing their land. However, there was resistance from some quarters.

In February 1918, an Executive Officer of the Cardiganshire War Agriculture Executive Committee visited Trenova, a six-acre smallholding in Beulah, some five miles north of Newcastle Emlyn, which was farmed by the Revd Daniel Dalis Davies. Davies was not present when the officer, the aforementioned Councillor John Jones JP of Cwmere, Felinfach, visited, but he received the latter's report with some dismay.

Jones had ordered Davies to plough two acres of his six-acre smallholding to grow crops instead of the grassland on which he was keeping some cows for milking. Jones was simply doing the work allotted to him by the Committee, which was operating Government policy; however, the order, repeated in many parts of the county and throughout Britain, appeared to some smallholders such as Davies as wholly unfair.

Letters were sent to the press by Dalis Davies and others who were particularly angry that the plough policy was only imposed on farms above ten acres in Carmarthenshire, while the limit was just five acres in Ceredigion. A meeting was arranged at the Lamb Inn in Newcastle Emlyn on 14 February 1918 to protest against the perceived injustice imposed on the county's *mân dyddynwyr* ['smallholders']. Among the speakers was E F George of Derllys, Cenarth, who, it was recorded in the CWAEC minute book, had persistently refused to plough some of his land.

A letter in Welsh from *'Chwarae Teg'* ['Fair Play'] published in *The Carmarthen Journal* on 22 February under the heading *'Gorthrwm Amaethyddol'* ['Agricultural Oppression'] set out the complaints of the Ceredigion smallholders against CWAEC and the farmers which dominated it. He pointed out that smallholders were not represented on CWAEC and that two farmers of military age had been appointed agents while applications from wounded soldiers who had been discharged from the Army had been rejected.

The protest by the smallholders soon dissipated, although it was sure to have soured relationships between the more substantial farmers and their lesser brethren.

*

By June 1916 food prices in Britain had risen by 60%, and this doubled over the ensuing two years. As indicated in the ditty at the beginning of the chapter, the increase in farm incomes led to accusations of war profiteering. Indeed, in March 1917, one local newspaper quoted an allegation that the war was not over because of 'Godly farmers who are praying for war to continue', such was the profit they had made during the war.

An off-the-cuff comment at a County Education Committee meeting caused a stir in the summer of 1917. When one farmer complained that farmers were expected to run at a loss, Councillor Evan Lima Jones, a chemist from Aberaeron, retorted:

> ...it is an astonishing statement to make that the poor farmers
> were suffering at the present time... To speak frankly, farmers
> were regarded as the locusts of the country.

The locust comparison was often used subsequently, despite the fact that, as one farmer pointed out, farmers grew food while locusts decimated it.

Food prices continued to rise and the Corn Production Act of 1917 gave the farmers a degree of certainty, with guaranteed prices for oats and wheat. Milk prices, as well as the quality of the product, were under constant scrutiny. In June 1918 milk vendors were fined by the Aberystwyth Petty Sessions Court for failing to comply with an order made by the local Food Committee that the price of milk should not be above 4 pence a quart. Among those prosecuted were some well-known farmers such as Daniel Jenkins, Bryncarnedd and Daniel Davies, Aberllolwyn. Although the bench's fine was lenient, the Aberystwyth and District Milk Sellers' Association decided to protest by withholding supplies of milk on that day. It was reported in the press that '...eighty per cent of the little children of the town went to school without having had any milk whatsoever. The scene in the street would have been amusing had the matter not been so serious. There was a procession of jug carriers [in those days milk was measured into customers' own receptacles from a churn] who returned in every case as they set out, and conveyed the bad news to their neighbours.' The dispute was soon resolved but it suggests that there was a genuine concern over profiteering by farmers and it also shows how controls on supply and prices were in operation by 1918.

*

One of the major complaints about farmers was the low wages paid to farmhands. On average, Ceredigion farmers paid lower wages than the farmers of every other county in Wales and it was reported that there were variations in wages in different parts of the county. To the north, an agricultural labourer might earn between £35 and £40 a year in 1918, while those to the south might only earn between £20 and £30. In 1917–18 several branches of the National Agricultural Labourers' and Rural workers' Union (NALRU) were formed, to press for an increase in wages and improvements in working conditions. The Llanilar branch demanded a minimum wage of £2 3s. a week, a ten-hour working day, a half-day holiday on Saturdays, payment at a rate of time-and-a-half for overtime and payment for Sunday working. One union organiser, T E Nicholas (see Chapter IX), claimed that: 'The Farmer's Union are opposing the Minimum Wage with all their usual bitterness. But the workmen are joining their Union fine.'

An investigation into the situation undertaken for the Government reported that the investigator '...met four branches and was struck by the hostility, amounting to almost hatred in some instances, shown by the men towards their employers... At one of the meetings, there was scarcely a single man of military age present, and it was explained that the local farmers had threatened to release for military service any farm-servant who dared to join the union.'

The investigator in question was Edgar Chappell, who was also, for a short period, the Editor of the journal *The Welsh Outlook*, and he took up the issue in the June 1918 edition:

Cardiganshire is generally regarded as one of the poorest counties of Wales and its farmers excuse themselves from paying a living wage to their employees by saying that they cannot afford to do so. This may have been true before the War, but in view of the recent Report issued by the Cardiganshire War Savings Committee it does not hold good today. The Committee reports that up to March 31, 1918, the War Savings Associations attached to Elementary Schools in the County had subscribed no less than £265,422 18s. 4d., while additional subscriptions amounting to £23,534 16s. 6d. had been made through other War Savings Associations. These investments apparently relate only to War Savings Certificates, and it is probable that a very large additional amount has been privately subscribed for War Bonds. The overwhelming proportion of the amounts mentioned was subscribed by farmers, and while we congratulate the County on its excellent record in regard to War savings, we would ask whether there is a satisfactory answer to the allegation that this record may have been achieved at the expense of the farm labouring classes. Farm workers in the County are wretchedly paid. Hired men and women work very long hours for very poor pay and in some parts of the County today married men receive cash wages as low as 9s. and 10s. per week. In our view it is dishonest for farmers to pile up investments in War Stock while they deny to their employees adequate means of subsistence. The Committee's Report demonstrates that Cardiganshire farmers are prospering, and we trust that the newly-found District Wages Committee will fix a minimum wage that will divert some of the farmers' profits into the pockets of the men and women whose labour they now exploit.

In the spring of 1918 the establishment by the Government of an Agricultural Wages Board, supported by District Wages committees, led to an improvement in wages and conditions but the agricultural depression of the interwar years saw farmers and farmhands alike suffer and the union branches in the county decimated.

*

Despite the criticism from several quarters, farmers did experience many difficulties during the war. There were labour shortages, the result of many farm labourers being recruited or conscripted into the armed services. Serving soldiers were released to work on farms for a maximum of 14 days at harvest times in 1915, with farmers able to apply to the local Labour Exchange for assistance. They were expected to pay the soldier 4 shillings a day, or 2 shillings and sixpence were the soldier to receive board and lodgings. J M Davies of Tymawr Farm, Ponterwyd was allowed to leave his posting with the South Wales Borderers to help out on the family farm, while other soldiers were allocated to farmers who had applied for assistance. No doubt many soldiers were relieved to spend time in the fields rather than serving on the front line.

Later in the war, German prisoners were allocated to farmers. It was reported by the Aberystwyth Agricultural Committee in July 1918 that the '...Food Production department was arranging for the supply of prisoners of war in gangs of ten, accompanied by two guards... Their hours were ten, excluding meal times, at 4*s* 6*d* per day.'

There was some opposition to the use of enemy labour, particularly in the Aberystwyth area, but when a complaint was made by Councillor C M Williams – a scourge of all things German – it was reported in the press that the council Chairman, J M Howell of Aberaeron, responded that he:

> ...regretted to find that feeling finding a response in the minds of anyone in that Council. There were at Monachty [Mynachty, Pennant] forty German prisoners. They passed through villages and towns and had been employed on the land, and in each place they were received with decent behaviour by the inhabitants and women and men had taken lunch out to them every day. (Hear, hear). It was one of the hopeful features of the future of Wales and a recognition of the fact that all peoples were of the same flesh and blood. The men on whose land the German prisoners worked said they worked far more conscientiously and satisfactorily than British soldiers sent as substitutes. They were anxious to do a good day's work and do it satisfactorily. People who spoke against those men were on the wrong track. It should be remembered that they were men.

Female labour was also available through the Women's Land Army, but this had limited influence on agricultural production in the county. Farmers' wives and daughters had in any case been an integral part of farming practice in the county over many centuries. It was they who milked the cows, fed the poultry and pigs and made butter and cheese, as well as managing the household and feeding the farmer and the farmhands. They were often the first to rise in the morning and the last to bed at night.

*

Despite the criticism of farmers, ultimately the 'plough policy' was successful in the county. Before the war, 60,076 acres of farmland were ploughed to grow wheat, barley, oats and potatoes, but this increased during the war to 68,628 acres. This was a creditable return for a county whose climatic conditions rendered the land more suitable for pasture than arable farming.

The war was, after all, being fought on two fronts. Firstly, the armed combat by armies in Europe and the Middle East, and secondly, the economic warfare which included the vital requirement to feed the people. Germany ultimately lost on both fronts: not only on the battlefield in 1918 but also as the naval blockade of its ports led to great food shortages or famine for much of its populace. It was calculated that over 400,000 Germans died from famine. This was not the case in Britain, despite the importation of food being disrupted by constant attacks by German U-boats on supply ships from North America and elsewhere. Shortages ultimately did lead to the rationing of some foodstuffs from January 1918 on, but there was no famine. In this respect, Ceredigion's agricultural community had played its part in securing the allied victory in November 1918 and, as one newspaper commented alongside the 'unpatriotic farmer ditty': 'we emphasise the fact that there are many farmers to whom such chaff could not apply, and who are among the most patriotic of all classes.'

VI

The Numbers Game: The Military Service Tribunals

By all means, the sick and incapable should be exempted, but those who are able should do their whack.
PRESS REPORT, JULY 1916

Send other people's sons to the Army, but don't send mine.
LETTER TO THE PRESS, JULY 1918

THERE WERE MANY tragic deaths during the war, but not all of these were on the battlefield. In 1916 a new development in the waging of the war by Britain, the compulsory conscription of young males, led to the death of two men from the south of the county, neither of whom had worn uniform. In March 1916, Thomas Evans, a 23-year-old farmer's son of Pledrog, Talgarreg, was found drowned in a brook near the farm with a 30lb stone tied round his neck. In the Coroner's Inquest Evans's mother stated that the '...deceased vexed a great deal about being called up to join the Army, and said more than once he would destroy his life rather than go. He lately heard it rumoured that general conscription would ensue, at which he was much alarmed.'

Evan James Jones – the son of David Cromwell Jones, a grocer and smallholder, and Priscilla Jones, a postmistress

85

– of Glasfryn, Tanygroes, near Cardigan, was exempted by the Cardigan Rural Military Tribunal in the spring of 1916 but the decision was overturned following a military appeal and he was expected to report to Brecon Barracks in May. His father became depressed and agitated and a doctor was called. Early one morning in April 1916 the father went to a barn and hung himself. The Tribunal which had conscripted his son subsequently reversed its decision, as Evan Jones was now the only remaining male member of the family who might run the business. In effect, the father had sacrificed himself in favour of his son.

Neither Thomas Evans's nor David Cromwell Jones's name appears on any war memorials, but they too were victims of the war.

*

The introduction of conscription was a consequence of mounting casualties and a decline in the number of volunteers. The other major countries involved in the war had long since introduced a system of conscription but Britain had resisted such a move on the grounds that it was against its liberal principles of freedom of choice. In 1915, however, there were calls, particularly by the War Office, for conscription to be introduced; otherwise, it was argued, the war would be lost.

The Government did not initially yield to the pressure, but in the summer of 1915 it organised a canvass of all eligible young men and subsequently introduced a 'Group Scheme' (also known as the 'Derby scheme' after its administrator Lord Derby) whereby men could 'attest' that they were willing to be called up. An eloquent London barrister, David Rhys, originally from Llanarth, travelled the length and breadth of the county in November and December 1915, holding well-attended meetings in towns and villages at which he urged young men to 'attest'.

Those who 'attested' were allowed to choose which service, regiment or unit they wished to join. Two brothers from Southgate, Penparcau, Evan James Thomas (a blacksmith) and Dyrus Thomas (a wheelwright), both attested. When called up in 1916, rather than be sent off to an infantry regiment, they chose to join the Royal Engineers, where they were able to make use of their engineering skills.

The numbers who 'attested' under the 'Group Scheme' proved insufficient and a Military Services Act was passed in January 1916. All voluntary enlistment came to an end and a process of compulsory military service or 'conscription' was introduced. All males were now deemed to have enlisted on 2 March 1916, as long as they were aged between 19 and 41, resided in Britain (excluding Ireland) and were unmarried or a widower on 2 November 1915. The age range was subsequently extended and by May 1916 married men were included.

A system of appeals tribunals was established to hear the cases of men who sought exemption from military service. There were four grounds for exemption:

– if it is expedient in the national interests that he should be engaged in other work, or, if he is being educated or trained for any other work, that he should continue; or
– if serious hardship would ensue owing to his exceptional financial or business obligations or domestic position; or
– ill health or infirmity; or
– conscientious objection to the undertaking of combatant service.

In Britain, of the 1.2 million single men deemed to be enlisted by the Act, 750,000 appealed against their conscription during the first 6 months. In Ceredigion itself, from March 1916 to the end of the war, over 6,000 men appealed – suggesting that many young men sought to avoid joining the armed services at any cost. Only a handful of these were conscientious objectors who refused to bear arms under any circumstances (for examples of these, see Chapter VIII). The remainder were clearly reluctant to give up their employment and presumably feared the consequence to life and limb of military service.

Those who sought exemption were often criticised in the press. The Swyddffynnon correspondent of *The Cambrian News* referred to them as 'the Fireside Battalions' or the 'Royal Standbacks', while the Lampeter correspondent of *The Carmarthen Journal* went even further:

> By hook or crook many suitable men for the army have been exempted in this district. The pains, suffering, ailments, and responsibilities the faint-hearted shirkers have invented are beyond belief, but have been efficacious to allow them to remain home, while other poor fellows are struggling with the foe for security of their country and homes. It is good news to hear that the authorities are going to investigate! Why so many have been exempted, and an end will be put to bogus cases. By all means, the sick and incapable should be exempted, but those who are able should do their whack. Many are snivelling in collieries, while others have gone to Canada or elsewhere to escape the Military Services Act. Their consciences ought to prick them when they see the noble deeds recorded in the papers of the patriotic heroes who nobly joined the army voluntarily, and not by compulsion.

*

There were three levels of Military Service Tribunal. The initial appeal for exemption was heard by local tribunals based on local authority areas. If that appeal failed then it was possible to make a further appeal to a county tribunal. There was also a central tribunal based at Westminster, but just a few problematic cases reached that stage, with only about 20 cases in all being referred to it from Ceredigion.

The local tribunals in Ceredigion were mostly made up of councillors, with the vast majority of the members in rural tribunals being farmers, while local small businessmen dominated the borough or town tribunals. The selection of members was made by the local authorities themselves and it appears there was some effort to ensure a reasonable geographical coverage. There were no women on the local or county tribunals, reflecting the patriarchal nature of the county's society at that time. It has been suggested that the difference between the appellants and the tribunal members was fundamentally one of age, but while it is true that tribunal members tended to be over 50 years old, there was also a class difference. The tribunal members were not paid and therefore only those with sufficient means, such as the more prosperous businessmen or farmers, could afford the time to serve. Whereas many appellants might be members of a chapel congregation, the tribunal members were more likely to be deacons – a clear divide in the community.

Although they were not party to the decisions of the tribunals, a military representative, usually a former officer, was present at the tribunal. This representative was able to ask questions and was often the most aggressive interrogator of appellants. He was supported by unofficial advisory committees, whose membership was not made public and which seemed to operate clandestinely. It appears that members of these committees were able to provide the military representative with information about the personal circumstances and character of an appellant. In one case a military representative referred to the habits of an appellant, whom he claimed spent much time drinking in a local inn, information which was probably provided by a local member of an advisory committee.

Also present at the tribunals were agricultural representatives, who could provide information on farming needs – an increasingly important factor. The tribunals were given clerical support, usually by the Clerk of a local or county council. Also present on some occasions were solicitors, acting on behalf of appellants.

It was not easy for a tribunal to make objective decisions based on sound legal principles. Whereas the county tribunal, as we shall see, comprised members with a legal background, this was not necessarily the case in the local tribunals. The guidance given to them by the Government was ambiguous and there was no formal training. Some tribunals placed the Army's interests at the forefront of their deliberations while others tended to take greater account of local needs. It is not surprising then that there was a marked inconsistency between different tribunals, both within and outside the county.

The most important term which coloured many of a tribunal's decisions was 'indispensable': in other words, was the appellant 'indispensable' to the operation of a business or farm, or for the well-being of a family? Farmers, for example, were encouraged to use substitute ploughmen who might work on several farms, thereby allowing a farmhand to be called up, as he could no longer claim to be indispensable. Out of the 52 cases heard by the Aberystwyth Rural Tribunal on 25 November 1916, three farmhands – Thomas Hugh Edwards, Pantygwyfol, and Thomas Henry Morgan, Pencarregfa, both of Llanilar, and R H Morgan, Bwlchglas, Tal-y-bont – were not exempted, with substitutes being provided to cover their work.

Very few were awarded absolute exemptions. Most were temporary and had to be renewed. There were some certified occupations which were considered to be indispensable in an agricultural community. This meant that blacksmiths could become 'badged men', exempt from military service. Jenkin Rees, the 19-year-old son of John Rees, a blacksmith in Aberaeron, was described as a 'shoeing smith and agricultural implement mechanic' at the Local Tribunal in March 1916. He was not exempted there, but the decision was reversed by the County Tribunal on the grounds that he was deemed to be a 'badged man'. However, the regulations were subsequently changed so an unmarried blacksmith would need to be aged 25 or over to claim exemption. Rees had to appear once again twelve months later, where his exemption was only extended to the end of April 1917, at which point he would be conscripted. There was a further hearing of his appeal soon after which was based on the grounds of the father's ill-health and the extent of the son's activities. Jenkin Rees was consequently exempted – although his brother, Evan Rees, was not so fortunate. When Evan reached his eighteenth birthday, his appeal was refused at both the Local and County Tribunals.

A 23-year-old saddler from Llanrhystud, Daniel Edwin Evans, was exempted in March 1916. He was supported by a petition signed by a hundred farmers who claimed that they would be unable to comply with the requirement of the Board of Agriculture to grow more crops were his services not to be available. His application stated that there were no other saddlers within nine miles of the village and his father was 76 years old and suffering from ill health. However, in June 1917, Evans was refused exemption by the Local Tribunal, which contended that his father could indeed undertake the work required. The County Tribunal ratified this decision. Evans became an air mechanic at the Royal Flying Corps School of Technical Training based at RAF Halton, but became ill and died in February 1918.

*

A tribunal's decisions could be subject to many influences. Both the local and county tribunals were open to the press and public, save for exceptional cases held in camera. Long reports on cases dealt with appeared in the press, although some newspapers did not include the name of the appellant.

The public who attended the meetings were not on the whole disinterested parties but rather family members or supporters whose attendance might well have influenced decisions, particularly where the appellant was well known locally. When popular Aberystwyth photographer Frank Culliford was given an exemption by the Aberystwyth Borough Tribunal in April 1916, the announcement was '...received with cheers'. Culliford claimed that he was the sole supporter of his mother, who was in her seventies, and his invalid brother, who assisted him in his work. However, in a similar case on the same day, Samuel Bluck – a 'cellarman and barman' of the Cross Foxes, Aberystwyth – failed in his attempt to gain an exemption. Bluck, whose mother was also in her seventies, received no sympathy from the military representative, Colonel Bonsall, unlike that given by him to Culliford. As it happens, the Bluck case is unusual in that he had already served with the Royal Artillery in France during 1916 but had returned home ill. Following his failure to gain an exemption, he was again posted to France with the Royal Garrison Artillery. He was struck and killed by a shell splinter in June 1917.

Influence was also exerted behind the scenes. There is some evidence of corruption elsewhere, with cash changing hands, but there is no proof of this occurring in Ceredigion. However, in close-knit communities where individuals were known to each other socially, perhaps through a chapel, and sometimes distantly related, a word in the ear of a tribunal member could influence a decision.

There is evidence of this in the diary of the Revd R J Rees, the Minister of Tabernacl Chapel, Aberystwyth (for Rees, see Chapter IV). Rees clearly assisted an insurance agent, David Jones of Cambrian Street. He visited Jones at his home on 6 February 1917 to discuss the latter's appeal for exemption to the Aberystwyth Borough Tribunal. According to Rees's diary, on the morning of the Tribunal on 9 February, he '…went to see a few members of tribunal re Ins. agent & was glad to find all our endeavours were successful.' Rees also attended the County Tribunal the following month, when Jones's appeal was challenged by the military. The exemption was reaffirmed.

The involvement of ministers of religion was common and many of the applications for exemption were written by a minister, particularly as the application forms were in English, a language in which many were not fluent in speech or writing. The application for exemption by a bacon curer, David Davies,

Gwarcefel, Llandysul, was clearly written by the Revd Ben Jones, Pantydefaid.

As the proceedings of the tribunals were often reported in full in the press, a number of quarrels and spats were recorded. In the Aberystwyth Borough Tribunal on 31 March 1916, the military representative, Colonel Bonsall, complained that the Clerk, John Evans, was '…acting rather as an advocate to try to get the men off.' Evans responded that he would not be dictated to: 'I am simply acting according to what I consider to be my duty in getting at the facts to enable the Tribunal to decide.'

Two members of the Aberystwyth Rural Tribunal were at odds on more than one occasion. Councillor John Richards, who farmed Tynpynfarch near Penrhyncoch, was, according to one report, 'one of the most useful public men in the district and an enterprising farmer'. His adversary on the Tribunal was Daniel Jenkins, who farmed Bryncarnedd on the road between Aberystwyth and Clarach. Richards sought exemption for his son and a farmhand and *The Cambrian News* reported on 3 March 1916 on the ensuing altercation:

> Mr Richards said he had put more land under the plough since the outbreak of war. He therefore claimed that he was doing his bit to feed the nation.
>
> Mr Daniel Jenkins – And to feed your own pocket as well.
>
> Mr Richards – Well, do you think I am a bigger fool than yourself?
>
> Mr Jenkins (warmly) – I object to that remark. I have two sons in the army, and I have to pay ineligible men to do their work. Mr Richards is here to save his own skin, and I am here suffering. Our cases are quite different.

At another meeting a fortnight later they continued their dispute:

> Mr John Richards – Where are we going to get the soldiers from?
>
> Mr Daniel Jenkins – From the small people of the county not from the large farmers.

Mr Richards (warmly) – And not from Mr Jenkins. His sons enlisted simply for the sake of a fortnight's holiday at the expense of John Bull.

The Chairman – Order, order.

Mr Richards – You call Mr Jenkins to order. I am on my defence. What right had Mr Jenkins to go to the military authorities to try and get his sons out.

Mr Jenkins – This is not the first time I have had this thrown to my face. I challenge Mr Richards to prove that I have tried to get my sons out of the army. I will not have these accusations directed against me.

Mr Richards – Do you get anything from the army in respect of your sons?

Mr Jenkins – Of course; but I never tried to get them out.

John Richards succeeded in obtaining exemption for his son, whom he claimed was a shepherd responsible for a thousand sheep. His farmhand, Lewis Richard Williams, was also exempted, but later in the war the latter's exemption was rescinded.

*

Whereas such behaviour might have been common in local tribunals, the county tribunal sessions were more ordered, reflecting the stature of the tribunal members. In Ceredigion, the County Council had initially proposed a membership made up of eleven Liberals (including several ministers of religion) and one Conservative, but following complaints, this was revised so that there were six Liberals and five Conservatives. There was no representation from the Labour movement, which at that time had little influence in the county and, as in the Local Tribunals, there were no women members. Unlike some counties, no member of the County Tribunal also served on the Local Tribunals. (For further details on the County Tribunal's membership, see the Appendix.)

The County Military Service Tribunal
(courtesy of Sally Leech)
Back: C M Williams (advisory committee); Joseph Evans, Llanfair Fawr; R S Rowland, Garth; D
Lloyd Lewis (Board of Agriculture representative); D C Roberts, Aberystwyth
Front: R Nancarrow, Ponthydygroes; Evan Evans, Aberystwyth; John Jones, Cwmere (chair); R J
R Loxdale, Castle Hill; E Lima Jones, Aberaeron
(This official photograph taken by H H Davies, Aberystwyth was probably taken in Aberystwyth
in 1918, with three prominent members, Sir Lawrence Jenkins, H M Vaughan and the Revd
John Williams, who lived in the south of the county, absent.)

The County Tribunal's members included a former Chief
Justice of the Calcutta and Bombay High Court, Sir Lawrence
Jenkins of Cilbronnau near Cardigan; the High Sheriff of the
county and man of letters, Herbert M Vaughan, Llangoedmor; a
lead mine manager, R R Nancarrow, Pontrhydygroes; a Baptist
minister, John Williams of Cardigan; together with several JPs.
Most of the eleven members were also county councillors and
there was good representation from the farming and business
communities. They were supported by a solicitor, Evan Evans,
Aberystwyth, who acted tirelessly as Clerk.

Meetings were held in several different locations around the county and the workload, together with the travelling time, proved onerous. The Tribunal dealt with about 2,000 cases in over 30 months, with the average sitting consisting of 28 cases a day. On 1 March 1917 at Lampeter, 43 cases were dealt with, and a further 36 on the following day.

Colonel Rennie Brewer and Major J R Williams as military representatives were also in attendance. The latter proved useful as he was a Welsh-speaker, so some questioning by the military of monoglot Welsh speakers was possible. There was also a representative acting on behalf of the Board of Agriculture. Whereas some members felt that Sir Lawrence Jenkins was the most appropriate member to chair the proceedings, the Liberal element had plotted prior to the first meeting to ensure that a farmer – the previously mentioned John Jones of Cwmere, Felinfach – would win the nomination.

The appellants were initially all single men, but when married men were also included in the amended Military Services Act of May 1916, the number of cases increased substantially. In Ceredigion, 40% of all appeal cases in the County Tribunal involved single men, with 58% of the cases involving married men and 1% widowers.

The cases dealt with in county tribunals were not only from appellants who had failed to gain exemption at local tribunals, but also appeals by the military representative against decisions taken by a local tribunal to exempt an appellant who would be, in the view of the Army, a suitable conscript. In Ceredigion, at the County Tribunal held on 9 May 1916, several appeals made by the military representative to the Tregaron Tribunal, David H Davies, were heard. The decision to exempt Evan Thomas Williams of Pontrhydfendigaid was upheld but the exemptions for Benjamin Evans, Blaenpennal, Thomas Edwards, Llwynbeudy, Swyddffynnon, and John Richard Thickens of Cwmystwyth were overturned. Of the 19 cases heard at that particular Tribunal, 11 of the appeals made by the military representatives were successful but the remainder were dismissed. It was not obvious in some cases why this was so, but generally a shepherd might expect to be exempted but not a cowman. Much depended too on individual circumstances, which varied from case to case.

There were disputes between the Local Tribunals and the County Tribunal – indeed, the Aberaeron Town Tribunal resigned en masse in protest against a decision taken by the County Tribunal in June 1916. The significance of this case is not clear, but it involved the appeal of a young baker, Henry Walter Hewitt, employed by Mary Ellen Lewis, who ran a bakery and confectionery business in Alban Square, Aberaeron. Hewitt was denied exemption by the Town Tribunal but he was temporarily exempted by the County Tribunal for a short period of two months, with no further right of appeal. Why this decision should have so vexed the Aberaeron Tribunal is not obvious but one can only conclude that it must have emanated from some obscure dispute. The matter was soon resolved, the resignations withdrawn and the Aberaeron Tribunal continued as before.

As with the Local Tribunals, there were cases in the County Tribunal whereby influence was applied unfairly. The case of J Teifion J Williams, a Cardigan architect and surveyor, was referred to in a brief memoir by H M Vaughan of his experience as a member of the County Tribunal published in the journal *Wales* in 1947. Williams had been exempted by the Local Tribunal for a short period, but he appealed to the County Tribunal for an extension. Williams's father, the Revd John Williams, was a member of that Tribunal. He stood down for the case hearing itself but had been active behind the scenes in canvassing support for his son among some of the other Tribunal members.

At the County Tribunal in August 1916, Teifion Williams argued that much building work in the Cardigan area would come to a stop were his services to become unavailable. He was quite impertinent in response to questions but his father had been successful in his canvassing and he was given a temporary exemption for six months. Eventually, by the time the period of his exemption came to an end, Teifion Williams had found employment in the Office of Works in London. He therefore avoided military service completely. The matter was well known locally and must have damaged the reputation of the father.

*

Despite the pressure to ensure the conscription of a good number of men, tribunals could be sympathetic to the needs of the farming community. Indeed, H M Vaughan wrote:

> Personally I could feel nothing but sympathy and sorrow for these poor men, especially for the elderly old-fashioned farmers whose quiet, orderly, useful existence of work and habit had thus been so rudely broken into and their intimate private affairs retailed in public.

The Army was anxious to recruit farmers' sons and farmhands since they often made good soldiers. A farmer's son from Ponterwyd, J M Davies, proved to be a good example of this. He subsequently wrote in his memoirs:

> We were healthy and strong boys and knew what a hard life was like. We grew up on solid food and were full of zest and energy. Most of us knew what carrying a gun was and we didn't need much guidance in this direction. I had killed enough foxes in the rocks of Gyfarllwyd near Devil's Bridge to know what 'rapid firing' entailed. [translation]

The Board of Agriculture's representative on the County Tribunal was J H Davies, Cwrt Mawr, Llangeitho, a prominent figure in many spheres of influence in the county. Apart from being the Registrar of Aberystwyth College (and later its

Principal), he was also the Chairman of the County Council in 1916–17. In March 1916 he wrote to the Board of Agriculture, seeking guidance on the number of men required on an agricultural holding:

> I think the Tribunal here would probably agree to some rough definition as to the relation between the number of men on a farm to the number of stock and the ploughed land. I was asked by the military representative whether I formed 'any idea' on this point but I thought it wiser not to commit myself. The farms in this county are small and have for many years been run with the minimum of labour. I do not think it possible to take any soldiers from the country districts without affecting the amount of production as people who are not normally occupied on the land always have to [be] turn[ed] to during harvesting operations and the potato seasons in order to help the farmer. This class has already been taken.

The response from the Board of Agriculture was short but to the point. It suggested that:

> ...it would be desirable that you should refrain, if possible, from expressing a general opinion as to the number of men required on an agricultural holding, as it depends, not only on the nature of the cultivation practised and the description of the land, but also on the local circumstances. For these reasons, it is almost impossible to lay down any hard and fast rule.

This was a reasonable approach but it was of no use to the tribunals, whose decisions would continue to appear arbitrary in some cases.

J H Davies undoubtedly influenced the deliberations of the County Tribunal and was canvassed by farmers seeking exemption for their sons or farmhands. On 25 March 1916, John Davies of Moelfryn Mawr farm, Bethania, wrote to J H Davies imploring him to speak on behalf of his son, Rees James Davies, who was to appear before the County Tribunal in Lampeter. The father farmed 168 acres but had been bedbound for about two months. He relied on his two sons, the elder of whom had been exempted but not the younger. He wrote again on 30 March, profusely thanking J H Davies for his intervention in the case, stating:

> According to the evidence of my son it was obvious that I would not have any hope of keeping him were it not for your defence of me. [translation]

J H Davies's interventions were not always successful. Daniel Williams of Newgate, Cilcennin, wrote to him on 25 March 1916 seeking his support for his son William, who had been exempted by the Aberaeron Rural Tribunal but was now subject a military appeal brought before the County Tribunal. William Williams's exemption was overturned and he was conscripted. In August 1916 he was killed at the Battle of Langemarck, while serving with the Machine Gun Corps.

Farmers were often accused of hypocrisy. W Jones-Edwards of Ffair Rhos wrote in his memoirs:

> I'll never forget that farmer from Bont who told me that it was my duty to enlist with the army. His sons were too young at that time, otherwise he said he would have forced them to go... I later heard that the farmer had bought another farm and that the two sons who had gone into business in London had since returned to farm it, and he had spent a fortune on solicitors to appear on their behalf at the tribunals. It is amazing how a man can change his opinion and principles when the boot is on the other foot.' [translation]

The farming community came under attack publicly, as exemplified in a letter by 'Cardi Bach' sent to *The Cardigan and Tivy-Side Advertiser* newspaper in July 1918. In a barrage of criticism of public bodies in the county, he referred specifically to those who served on the Tribunals:

...where they take care to shelter eligible young men from the Army. "Send other people's sons to the Army, but don't send mine" is their motto.

In mid 1917 an attempt was made to manage the competing claims of the military and the agricultural community. In effect, this meant that no more men engaged in agriculture were to be recruited, except by the consent of the county's War Agricultural Executive (see Chapter V), who were charged with issuing 'protection cards' to those whom they considered to be indispensable in food production.

The situation changed once more in the spring of 1918, following the massive offensive by the German Army on the Western Front which nearly proved fatal to the Allies. There was a desperate need for more men and a Royal Proclamation was issued on 20 April 1918, by which Exemption Certificates for youths born between 1895 and 1899 were withdrawn. It was expected that this would lead to the enlistment of 30,000 additional men and each county was given a target. In Ceredigion this was 425. Many of those who lost their exemption rights worked in agriculture but, in the event, most in the county were in fact given temporary exemptions until December 1918. By the summer, the tide had turned against the Germans, largely because of the influx of fresh American troops, at a rate of about 300,000 a month, which boosted the Allies. Although it was not known at that time, the new exemptions stretched until after the war had come to an end, with the armistice being signed on 11 November 1918.

*

In general, the conduct of the Military Service Tribunals was much criticised. The War Office complained that they were too sympathetic, leading to many eligible men being exempted, while the Board of Agriculture argued that food production was imperative and young farmers and farmhands required to achieve this were wrongly sent to the Army. The tribunals were in an unenviable position. Whereas the War Office and the Board of Agriculture dealt with statistics, the tribunals had to deal openly with individual men. Their decisions were of great consequence to the men whom they refused to exempt, together with their families and their communities.

One specific case led to bitter comments on the tribunal system by the Llanarth local correspondent to *The Cambrian News*. Jenkin Davies, a popular postman and active member of Pencae Congregational Chapel, Llanarth, had been killed near Ypres in June 1917, aged 38. The correspondent wrote:

> When the sad news was received, all who knew him felt a deep pang of sorrow, for he was, owing to his good, kind, and affable disposition, universally loved. When it was known the Tribunal had passed him for the army, a general cry of condemnation was heard. There was none of the soldier in him mentally or physically. Being a monoglot Welshman he suffered when in training.
> Before he was called to the army he served as one of the postal messengers delivering letters in outward district. A more faithful, trustworthy official could not be found. The whole district mourns his loss. Much sympathy is felt with his sister, with whom he made his home.

H M Vaughan himself commented later on the tribunal system, which he described as a '...callous and unfair method employed in 1916 of dealing with our manhood as it were in a lump, covering extreme youth to middle age.' He and other tribunal members showed much empathy with many of the appellants, which reflected a prevailing ambivalent attitude to the war and its consequences.

VII

Families in Wartime

*...how I would like again to strike a bayonet
through & through a dirty German & tell him
with each stroke "for Dai – for Dai"...*

LETTER FROM CAPTAIN TALFRYN JAMES, 1916

*...I hope that you won't be going to the trenches
or I don't know what I would do, but I have nothing
to do now but to pray for you dear child and hope that
everything will become all right again.*

LETTER FROM RACHEL DAVIES TO HER SON, C.1916

WHEN DAVID EVANS, the postman at Cribyn near Lampeter, received a letter from the War Office for delivery to a local family, he would don his top hat and coat and walk through the village to deliver the letter, which more than likely contained bad news about the fate of a son or husband. Those who saw him on the road prayed that he would not be calling at their homes. In April 1918 he himself received such a letter, with the distressing news that his own son, Jacob Evans, had been killed in battle.

At the end of August 1918 Mrs Annie Blair of Cambrian Gardens, Aberystwyth was also the recipient of a letter from the War Office, which stated that her husband, Private Horace Blair, had been killed in action in France. His three-month-old son, William Horace, had been born while his father was away at the front. The little boy was never to see his father and although Horace Blair had been sent a photograph of him, he was never able to experience holding his own child in his arms.

As well as the grief, a widow with a baby would have found it difficult to manage financially under such circumstances. Annie Blair would have received a war widow's pension of a minimum of 13 shillings and 9 pence a week, together with a 5-shilling allowance for her child, but such pensions provided by the state only covered the basic cost of raising a family without a breadwinner.

Annie Blair was one of the 240,000 British widows who had lost their husbands as a result of the war, although it appears that only a few of the casualties from Ceredigion were married men with children. It was more likely that it was a parent, like the Cribyn postman, or sibling, rather than a wife or a child, who suffered the grief of losing a loved one.

*

Family members informed of a soldier's death were usually unable to grieve over a coffin and witness a burial as bodies were, as a rule, not repatriated and the soldier would be buried near to where he died. In some cases, bodies were not even recovered from the battlefield and had no known graves. Sailors were as a norm buried at sea, or their bodies were never recovered following the sinking of ships by U-boats or mines.

There were some exceptions. David Morris Jones of Beulah, a 16-year-old sailor, was drowned when his ship, the SS *Canganian*, was sunk by a mine near Scapa Flow in November 1916. His body was recovered on the Scottish coast but he was not identified and was buried locally. However, his coat bore the name 'Ben Davies, draper, Newcastle Emlyn' and through the local press he was identified and his family informed. His body was exhumed and reburied in the family grave at Beulah on 9 December 1916.

As a rule, families were not allowed to visit their injured sons at the front but some, usually from among the well-to-do, were able travel to the continent to see them at hospitals well behind the lines if it was safe to do so. Sub-lieutenant W H K 'Billy' Owen of Llanbadarn Fawr, a gifted Cambridge University student who had enlisted in August 1914, was severely wounded at the battle of Loos in September 1915. He was transferred to a hospital in Rouen and his parents were informed of this by telegram, but also told that they could not visit him. However, by some means (probably through contacts made by his father, the prominent local solicitor W P Owen), Owen's mother Ethel was allowed to travel to France to see her son. She arrived in Rouen in time to embrace him before, it is said, he died in her arms. His final words were *'Gwell angau na chywilydd'* ['Better death than dishonour'], the motto of the Welsh Regiment in which he had served.

The effect on mothers like Ethel Owen of losing a son was particularly traumatic. When Dafydd ('Dai Wern') Jones, the popular son of Thomas and Margaret Jones, Wern Farm, Llanio, Llanddewi Brefi, was killed in the bloody battle for Mametz Wood in July 1916, his mother received numerous letters of condolence.

Both Dafydd Jones and Lilian Howell of Aberaeron studied at Aberystwyth College before the war and they may have been sweethearts. Lilian wrote to his mother following his death:

> I had prayed so much for him to be saved. When we heard about some major battle my first thought was "Is Dai safe" and a small prayer always went with all the others. During the big battle in Mametz I had a weird sensation. I remember one day especially when reading the paper, I was forced to give up by the feeling that came over me. I thought my heart had stopped due to the size and depth of my feeling. In retrospect I saw that it was the day Dai was killed. [translation]

One other letter from Captain Talfryn James, who had served with Jones, expressed his hatred of the Germans:

> ...how I would like again to strike a bayonet through & through a dirty German & tell him with each stroke "for Dai – for Dai"...

Another letter by an old friend of her son, John Williams, Dolyfelin, was more typical. He stated:

> The only consolement [sic] you can have is that poor Dai died for a good cause and that it was the will of God that it should be so.

Likewise David Williams of Treherbert referred in his letter to the family to the 'mysteries of providence'.

What effect such correspondence might have had on Elizabeth Jones is hard to gauge, but she kept all the letters, together with her son's name tag, which had been recovered from the battlefield.

For most parents it was their religious beliefs and the support of chapel or church, together with relatives and friends, which sustained them at a time of immeasurable grief, rather than any concept of dying for King and country.

Some were profoundly affected by their loss for the rest of their lives. William Jones-Edwards of Ffair Rhos wrote in his autobiography of the sorrow of Mrs Jenkins, known as 'Mami Siencyn', of Pontrhydfendigaid, whose son was killed at Pilkem Ridge in 1917. Although she continued to attend Carmel Chapel, her previously melodious voice was no longer to be heard during the hymn singing.

*

Whereas many letters from those serving in the armed forces have survived, there are only a few extant letters from family members sent to sons, husbands or brothers at the front. The most poignant of these have a note on the envelope with words to the effect that the soldier had been killed in action and the letter was being returned to the sender.

David Davies of Llandysul served with the Monmouthshire Regiment during the war. He kept the letters sent to him by his mother Rachel. Apart from local gossip, his mother wrote of her concerns about his well-being:

> Dear son I think a lot about you day and night. I am afraid you are not getting food properly or a change of clothes. I would like you to have your parcels and letters on time. I hope that you won't be going to the trenches or I don't know what I would do, but I have nothing to do now but to pray for you dear child and hope that everything will become all right again. [translation]

And while she was worried about her son, he was worried about his mother. But her response was:

> I am having a wondrous strength that I think it is true that God is listening to your prayers because I am calm and I sleep well every night, better than I did throughout the winter, don't worry about me. [translation]

Davies survived.

*

During the war, whereas most mothers kept the home or, in the case of farmers' wives, also worked on the farm, some single women found employment as shop workers or maid servants, or undertook various clerical duties. However, some women were anxious to support the war effort directly.

Gwen Stephen from Lampeter was a skilled seamstress who joined the Women's Army Auxiliary Corps in 1915. She worked at several factories at Filton near Bristol and Farnborough in Hampshire which built warplanes. Her skills were put to good use in the sewing of the canvas wings for the light and rather flimsy aeroplanes built at that time.

Other young women were employed in Red Cross hospitals, either as nurses or as largely untrained assistants known as VADS (Voluntary Aid Detachment). The most formidable nurse from the county was Emilie G Evans, who was the Matron of the Aberystwyth Infirmary at the outbreak of the war. In October 1914 she was recruited to run the Welsh hospital based at Netley, near Southampton. This was a large wooden structure located, together with many English 'county' hospitals, in the grounds of the Royal Victoria Hospital. It was described as a '…"temporary" hospital with all the appearance of a well settled establishment'. One commentator observed:

Matron Emilie Evans

Rachel Davies
(courtesy of Enid Gruffudd)

But how do you know it is Welsh? There can never be any doubt. One has only to pass the sisters on the corridor, to hear the orderlies. Welsh faces, Welsh eyes and Welsh voices stamp the Hospital as Welsh.

Emilie Evans returned to Aberystwyth after the war and ran a private nursing home in Portland Street.

Some nurses served overseas. The Aberystwyth District Nurse, Gwenllian Morris, served in Red Cross field hospitals in France before being struck down by diphtheria. At that time, before widespread vaccination, this could be a fatal disease but she recovered and was soon volunteering to serve on the Serbian front. She was posted to a hospital at a town called Požarevac, where typhoid was rife. When the Bulgarian Army overran the town, she was captured and imprisoned in a town near Belgrade. She survived and after the war continued her nursing career in Somerset. Another young nurse, Ella Richards from Lampeter, was not so fortunate: she died of pneumonia in Salonika in October 1918. She was the only female casualty from the county who died while serving abroad.

Also in Salonika was Beryl Morgan from Aberystwyth, who acted as a superintendent of cooking at a large Canadian hospital. Other young women entertained the troops. A well-known local singer, Sophie Rowlands of North Parade, Aberystwyth, undertook a concert tour of hospitals in Malta while Nesta Morgan, also from Aberystwyth, sang to the troops in France. She wrote home in January 1917:

There are four of us, each contributing to providing musical entertainments at the different Y.M.C.A. huts. One can hardly realise what a comfort music is to the men. There is a special hut where they rest for a few hours on their way to and from the trenches. Mud-stained and tired, one wonders whether they can sing and yet when the order comes – some time during a solo – they march away humming the latest chorus quite cheerfully and bravely. This is the spirit which makes one very proud to be "British". Last night our concert hall – the third floor of a mill

– was lit by half-a-dozen candles. There were 400 men – you can imagine how all the available space was taken up – resting after being eight months in trenches. They were the most appreciative audience we have sung to.

In France later that year was Maud Jepson of Marine Terrace, Aberystwyth, who was proudly reported to have been the first from the town to be recruited as a woman clerk by the Women's Army Auxiliary Corps. She had been appointed following an interview in Liverpool, where the other successful candidates appeared to her to be a 'superior type of girl'.

Many women who could not serve directly were particularly anxious to support the war effort at home, by any means possible. Often organised by middle-class or gentry ladies, they volunteered to undertake a variety of tasks. The Darllenfa Sewing Circle organised by Miss Catherine Powell Evans in Penparcau sent flannel shirts, socks, bed jackets, balaclava helmets and mittens to soldiers at the front. There were similar groups in Aberarth and New Quay. Such support was sometimes channelled to the front through unofficial arrangements, such as those made by old soldier Sergeant-Major T R Fear of Aberystwyth, who organised a constant supply of parcels to serving soldiers. The appreciation of this by soldiers and sailors was obvious from letters of thanks published in local newspapers.

Doris W Stapledon, wife of the famous botanist Professor (later Sir) George Stapledon, organised a hoeing gang of women, consisting chiefly of girls from the College and the organiser's own friends. Despite early scepticism expressed by local farmers, the gang began work in June 1916 and succeeded in hoeing 790 rows of swedes, averaging 160 yards each, in a matter of six weeks.

In the spring of 1917, it was reported that the young women of Mydroilyn had been planting vegetable seeds in a 'war plot' in the village, with the aim of selling the produce and donating the proceeds to the local soldiers' funds.

The Women's Land Army was also active in the county, though not in great numbers. It was recorded that 130 members of the Land Army had worked on the land in Ceredigion, but only 20 of these came from the county itself. Some farmers were dubious of their contribution, particularly the middle-class young women who were not used to farm work. The farmers' wives and daughters had been trained from an early age to undertake all manner of tasks on the farm, as well as household chores, and worked for most of the day. However, it was reported that Land Army women objected to working such long hours and to undertaking non-agricultural chores. A Government inspector recorded:

> In a few instances farmers have required the uniformed labourers [Land Army women] to wash floors, cook, nurse babies, and to do household work, and they have been rather perplexed at being met with a blank refusal.

*

Although women played their part in the home 'war effort', there was also an important contribution by men who were not in the armed services.

There were an estimated 27,000 males living in the county at the outset of the war. If about 5,500 were recruited to the Army or associated services at some point during the war (see Appendix), there were over 20,000 males who remained in the county. Most of these were either too young or too old to enlist, but there were many men of military age who did not serve. These included those who were medically unfit for service or had been exempted by the Military Service Tribunals because they were employed in work which was considered to be valuable for the war effort (see Chapter VI). A large proportion of those living in rural areas were farmers or skilled farmhands, while in the towns those who ran small but useful businesses were often exempted.

Prior to conscription, the young men who avoided recruitment were often accused of being 'shirkers' or 'slackers' and such comments were still prevalent about those who, following the introduction of conscription from 1916, were exempted on what some considered to be spurious grounds. The few miners who worked in the lead mines in the north of the county were a target for the provocative Aberystwyth councillor Dr Harries, who declared in 1917 that: 'One man could wheel to London in a barrow in a month all the lead produced in the county.' He also complained of '...farmers' sons who took out gun licences and were wasting their time in shooting pheasants.'

In February 1917 a new National Service Scheme was introduced, mainly to manage the supply of manpower and direct it to where it was most needed, such as munition factories. Under this scheme every man (and later women) between 18 and 61 could volunteer for 'national work'. If selected, they would be sent to an appropriate place of employment and paid a minimum of 25 shillings a week plus subsistence and travelling allowances.

Under the scheme, Commissioners were nominated and for Wales John Rowland (later Sir John Rowland), a native of Tregaron and a former secretary to Lloyd George, was appointed. It was said that he tended to favour Tregaron men for any public appointment and, indeed, he nominated Morgan Morgan, Neuadd, Tregaron, as the Sub-Commissioner for the county. As described in Chapter IV, during the spring of 1917, the Revd R J Rees was recruited to speak at scores of public meetings to seek support for the scheme. Despite much enthusiasm, the scheme proved unwieldy and it was brought to an end following the fundamental reorganisation of the National Service Department in August 1917. It was reported that 270,000 men and women registered under the scheme across Britain, but we have no separate figures for Ceredigion.

*

Apart from letters received from husbands, sons or brothers at the front, families relied on newspapers for information. Weekly local papers such as the *Cardigan and Tivy-Side Advertiser*, *The Welsh Gazette* and *The Cambrian News* contained news on the progress of the war, references to (and often photographs of) local members of the armed services and lists of casualties. Welsh-language newspapers such as *Y Faner* were also read but increasingly England-based daily newspapers with more up-to-date information became more popular. There was also an environment in which gossip, rumour and speculation was rife. John Evans, the Headmaster of the Boys' Council School in Cardigan, wrote in the school log book on 17 April 1917 of rumours in the town that his second son had been killed in France and that another son's ship had been torpedoed. He commented ruefully: 'These rumours completely upset me this day & I did but little work at school.' Luckily, neither rumour was true.

In many ways the activities of those who stayed at home, both male and female, were useful in keeping up morale. They contributed to the war effort in a variety of ways, but the fear of bad news from the continent could never have been far from their minds.

VIII

Schools in Wartime

In 'our country' every boy and girl, every man and woman,
has a share: in serving 'our country' every one must take part.
The symbol of the unity of the scattered peoples who belong to
'our country' is the Union flag. That unity shelters us
and keeps the British Empire together.

PATRIOTISM: SUGGESTIONS TO LOCAL EDUCATION AUTHORITIES AND
TEACHERS IN WALES REGARDING THE TEACHING OF PATRIOTISM, 1916

I have a serious objection to taking life and I have been preaching
that for the last ten years. I believe that international disputes
could be settled without the shedding of blood.

T BRYN JONES'S APPEAL FOR EXEMPTION FROM WAR SERVICE, 1916

THE WAR UNQUESTIONABLY impinged on the lives of children,
particularly those with fathers or brothers in the armed services.
The absence of such role models, despite their depiction as
heroes, must have influenced a child's development. Those
children who lost close relatives would have been deeply
distressed and family structures disturbed.

The behaviour of older children might be seriously affected.
The Headmaster of Cardigan Boys' Council School recorded
in the school log book in June that one boy's attitude to
schoolwork was 'indifferent'. His father was at sea and his

Aberaeron Council School: Standards III & IV, 1914
(courtesy of Archifdy Ceredigion Archives)

mother an invalid and therefore '...the boy to a great extent does much as he likes.'

From the evidence in school log books, school attendance seemed to be a more important indicator of a school's success in the minds of head teachers and the education authorities than the actual quality of education. Although this was not new, children in rural areas were often absent from school when the hay harvest, potato digging or sheep shearing were in full swing. There were absences too because of illnesses such as whooping cough, measles, scarlet fever and diphtheria – for example, several pupils at Aberaeron Council School were absent in March 1915 as a result of an epidemic of German measles. All schools were closed for two months at the end of the Autumn term of 1918 because of the deadly 'Spanish flu' influenza pandemic which had spread throughout the world.

In the early part of the war, it was business as usual in the county's schools. The syllabus in elementary schools remained the same, apart from some adjustment to geography lessons in some schools where, following guidance from the Director of Education, the geography of Europe was emphasised. In Aberystwyth Boys' Council School, the Headmaster wrote in the school log book in September 1914:

> In Geography the top class St[andards] 6 & 7 will this year study Europe especially those parts that are more intimately connected with the Great War.

Attention was also given to certain historical events. Pupils at Aberystwyth Girls' Council School were given a lesson on the Battle of Trafalgar on Trafalgar Day in October 1914, in which emphasis was placed on '…its results, and the meaning of the British Navy to our National life and Imperial influence…' Meanwhile 'a special study of the British Empire [was] to be made in Standard VII'.

Such lessons were a matter for the headmaster or headmistress to implement, but by 1916 a greater emphasis on the teaching of 'patriotism' was encouraged by the Welsh Department of the Board of Education. This centred on activities associated with St David's Day, which had become a major event in the school calendar from 1911 onwards.

In 1914, prior to the war, a bilingual pamphlet was circulated by the Welsh Department of the Board of Education suggesting ways in which schools and colleges might celebrate St David's Day. This was distributed widely and its suggestions adopted by most schools. It referred to the 'higher ideals of patriotism, of inspiring richer conceptions of citizenship, of kindling, in the minds of old and young alike, a keener sense of personal responsibility and of public duty.' There is reference to 'love of country' and although this is not defined, it implies that the country in question is Wales rather than Britain:

Wales needs today, as she has ever done, men and women who love their nation and, like the patriot of former days, are prepared to make sacrifices in order to serve her; then, indeed, will the observance of St David's Day in the schools and colleges of '*yr hen wlad*' be not merely justified but desirable on the widest possible scale.

This appeal was followed by suggestions for a programme of events and activities to be undertaken on St David's Day, including processions, tableaux, telling stories, singing and possibly a school eisteddfod.

The following year, with the war very much in mind, a similar pamphlet was produced and 25,000 copies distributed. This emphasised the need to tell the story of two Welsh warrior heroes. These, somewhat incongruously, were Owain Glyndŵr and Sir Thomas Picton. The former had fought for Welsh freedom, while the latter was one of the heroes of the Battle of Waterloo. Owain's enemy was the King of England while Waterloo saw the French defeated, with the intervention of Prussian soldiers on the British side proving crucial. Whether this irony was recognised by teachers in 1915 is not known, but certainly the darker side of Picton's career, which involved slavery and brutality (including the torture of a young woman), would not have been mentioned – nor Wellington's comment that Picton was "a rough foul-mouthed devil as ever lived".

With the armed forces suffering from mounting casualties and a lack of volunteers, the introduction of conscription in early 1916 brought with it a drive for a greater patriotic spirit from the entire population, including children. A new bilingual booklet was published by the Welsh Department of the Board of Education called *Patriotism: Suggestions to Local Education Authorities and teachers in Wales regarding the teaching of patriotism.*' The tone of this publication was quite different to that of the previous pamphlets. The section in the Welsh language concentrated mainly on St David's Day and Wales while the English parts contained more on the role of Wales as part of the wider British Empire. Although not stated as such, it might be said that the former section represented '*Hen Wlad fy Nhadau*' and the red dragon and the latter 'God Save the King' and the Union Jack.

The Welsh section led with the *raison d'être* of the booklet:

> Leading the children of Wales to respect the sublime and love the beautiful; to be willing to sacrifice self and to reach out completely for purity and truth; to cultivate that strong commitment to duty – to neighbour and to country – which underlies all pure patriotism; to support the young in wishing to become single-minded and useful members of society, and worthy sons and daughters of the country to which they belong... No nation can rest on what it has once been, and the celebration of the Festival of a Nation is not worthy of the name unless it can create in the citizens of the future a deep feeling of affection for the land of their fathers, as well as a true appreciation of the things that matter in the life of a nation. [translation]

It then lists the things that all Welsh children should know about St David's Day. This is followed by an essay on Welsh historical events and how modern Welsh children should seek to accomplish greater achievements than those in the past.

The English section locates Wales as an integral part of the British Empire, as set out in the introduction written by Alfred T Davies, Permanent Secretary of the Welsh Department of the Board of Education:

> As belonging to the oldest part of that Empire, Wales may fitly take a leading share in inculcating in her children right conceptions of Patriotism, using the term in its widest sense, and the general observance of St David's Day in Wales offers a great opportunity for suitable following up and emphasizing the lessons given on that day.

A further essay defines 'patriotism' and in particular what 'our country' means:

In 'our country' every boy and girl, every man and woman, has a share: in serving 'our country' every one must take part. The symbol of the unity of the scattered peoples who belong to 'our country' is the Union flag. That unity shelters us and keeps the British Empire together... This then is 'our country' to which we are proud to belong; this is the land which we must be willing to serve: these the liberties we should be eager to defend, even to the last drop of blood.

This was followed by sections entitled 'What our country has done for us', 'How can we serve our country' and 'Why our country needs our service, especially at the present time'. Also included are suggestions on how to celebrate St David's Day. One of these was that a local 'Roll of Honour' be '...read aloud and displayed to the children and all information possible given to them as to the whereabouts and doings of the old scholars who have gone to fight in the Great War.'

The booklet ends with an essay entitled 'True patriotism and false patriotism', in which 'true patriotism' is explicitly contrasted with the false patriotism of Germany and its allies. Instances of brutality, such as the treatment of the Belgians and the sinking of the *Lusitania*, are described as '...inhuman – murder not war – and a lasting disgrace to the countries which have perpetrated them... No nation is really great whose Patriotism takes the form of hating other nations'.

St David's Day in 1916 was celebrated in several different ways in the county's schools but many of the recommendations made by the Board of Education were implemented. In Aberystwyth Boys' Council School, playlets entitled *Yr Union Jack* and *Joinio'r Fyddin* ['Joining the Army'] were performed alongside recitations entitled *Cariad at Gymru* ['Love for Wales'] and *Cymry bychain ydym* ['Little Welshmen are we'].

In Pontrhydfendigaid school it was recorded that: 'The Recruiting and sacrifices made by all classes to defend their country were dwelt upon and children asked to bring lists of volunteers from the District and given as homework.' Such exercises, as suggested by the Board of Education, led to the compilation of Rolls of Honour which were then displayed in schools.

Schools were henceforth encouraged to teach 'patriotism' as part of the ordinary syllabus. In the Cardigan Girls' Council School, the Headmistress recorded in the school log book on 6 March 1916:

> In accordance with the request of the Cardiganshire Education Committee and indirectly with that of the Board of Education, patriotism will be taught during the first half hour, on the first Monday of each month in future.

In 1917 the same school purchased a photograph of Jack Cornwell, a 16-year-old boy who had been awarded a posthumous Victoria Cross for his gallantry at the naval Battle of Jutland, and raised funds to have it framed and displayed in the school.

*

Apart from a degree of indoctrination, school pupils – particularly in the towns – were expected to undertake specific tasks to support the war effort, mostly during school hours. As early as October 1914, the girls of the Aberystwyth National School were charged with knitting mittens for the soldiers. It was recorded that 100 mittens and 5 scarves had been completed by the end of the month. In October 1915 Major Mathias, the recruiting officer for the county, brought 600 War Office recruiting letters to the Aberystwyth Council School and the boys of Standard VII spent most of the day writing addresses on envelopes.

Most schools had a garden where potatoes and other vegetables were grown. In March 1918 it was reported that Aberystwyth County School had constructed a garden of 530 square yards. 1,196 lbs of potatoes had been sold to the pupils at a penny a pound and 72 lbs kept for seed. It was said that '...much difficulty was experienced in getting the boys to work after school hours and compulsion had to be used.' However, a new scheme whereby pupils had been given plots to cultivate themselves had proved successful.

Food shortages led to a Food Economy Campaign, which was embraced by pupils of Aberystwyth Girls' Council School. All children were asked to sign a pledge:

> We hereby pledge ourselves
> 1. to eat our food slowly and to chew it well
> 2. to eat as little bread as possible
> 3. to waste no food at all
>
> So that the supply of wheat may last as long as possible and thus the work of the enemy submarines may be made of no avail.

Every child complied and each was duly presented with a purple ribbon.

Children were also used to collect fruit. Several hundredweight of horse chestnuts were collected by Cardigan boys in the autumn of 1917 and packed off by rail for use in the manufacture of cordite for armaments. This exercise was soon discontinued as the acetone produced proved to be of an inferior quality. Under the patronage of Lady Jenkins of Cilbronnau, the same children collected over a thousand pounds of blackberries which, in September 1918, were sent to a factory in Cardiff which manufactured jam for the soldiers.

In rural areas, eggs were collected in great numbers. It was reported in February 1917 that nearly ten thousand eggs had been collected in the Tal-y-bont area in the north of the county since April 1915, with major contributions coming via Tal-y-bont, Taliesin, Elerch (Bont-goch) and Rhydypennau (Bow Street) schools. These eggs had been sent to base hospitals and to the Welsh hospital at Netley.

Schoolchildren were also encouraged to save through the War Savings Committees established in 1916, which operated through the county's schools. The Cardiganshire War Savings Committee reported that up to 31 March, 1918, the War Savings Associations attached to elementary schools in the county had subscribed no less than £265,422. 18s. 4d., while additional subscriptions amounting to £23,534. 16s. 6d. had been made through other War Savings Associations.

Aberystwyth Girls' Council School, which had about 300 pupils, recruited 163 subscribers by March 1917, with total savings of £376. 18s., while the pupils of Cardigan National School had saved £1,046 by the end of the war. Obviously this money had come from parents who could spare some cash, and it is important to note that these were not *donations* to the cause but *savings* which could be withdrawn at a later date. Nevertheless, the savings provided much-needed funds for the Government and encouraged thrift and a sense of individual and community contribution.

Richer parents – particularly the more prosperous farmers – purchased war bonds, which were a lucrative investment as well as affording the investor with the personal satisfaction of supporting the war effort. The sums raised through these and other means were substantial for a county noted for its parsimony, and one which was among the poorest in Britain.

*

Some teachers enlisted at the outset of the war. The veteran soldier John Thomas, head of Aberporth National School, joined up at the age of 58 and was employed during the war at the recruiting office in Carmarthen. Lieutenant David Jones, an assistant teacher at Cwrtnewydd School before the war, and Private Edwin Griffiths Jones, the geography master at Aberystwyth County School, were among the 2,000 British teachers killed during the war.

Many other teachers remained in post until they were called up following the implementation of conscription. In

March 1916, the county's Director of Education, Jenkin James, claimed that he only wished to retain the services of four of the 42 male teachers of military age in the county. He argued that one assistant teacher at Aberystwyth Boys' Council School should not be conscripted, claiming that:

> The school was the largest in the county and it was necessary that there should be one male teacher in addition to the Headmaster. The other teacher would be allowed to go. Experience showed that female teachers could not manage boys in the upper standards.

Some teachers were conscientious objectors and two of these were involved in bitter disputes. In February 1916 Dr Daniel James Davies, a teacher at Aberystwyth County School, was exempted from military service by the Aberystwyth Borough Military Service Tribunal on the grounds that he was a conscientious objector. He was given that status for as long as he remained in his post. Over the ensuing two years, some of the school's governors made several attempts to dismiss him, an act which would have left him open to conscription.

Ironically, Davies was a modern languages teacher who taught German and had been awarded a doctorate by Marburg University in Germany before the war. He was popular with the pupils, even if his subject was not. One pupil, J R Richards, who later became the Bishop of St Davids, recalled that he and his fellow-classmates wrote

D J Davies

on the cover of their German exercise books, '*Gott strafe Deutschland*' ['God punish Germany'].

Davies was a long-standing pacifist and an active member of the Unitarian chapel in the town. In September 1916 a proposal by C M Williams, a governor who was also a veteran local councillor and sometime Mayor of Aberystwyth, to dismiss Davies was narrowly defeated. Williams claimed that he did not oppose Davies because he was a conscientious objector but argued that Davies had a negative influence on the children, who considered him to be a coward. One governor argued in favour of Davies, stating that if he were to be dismissed, Davies would be forced to enlist and might be court-martialled and then shot. He asked rhetorically:

> Would Mr Williams say "Serve him right"?' I am sure none of us would dare say that.

'I should,' was the response of another governor, Mrs Hannah Richards. She went on to say, 'A man who will not help his country in its hour of need is not worth considering.'

This was, then, the rather severe view of a former teacher from north-east Wales who had married a local farmer from Capel Seion.

Although Davies survived that vote, in November 1917 he was not so fortunate. Williams's proposal to dismiss him was passed by five votes to four. The decision was greeted with dismay by correspondents to the local press. To one it was a 'grievous scandal', while the National Union of Teachers wrote: 'Unfortunately, Prussianism is not confined to Prussia'. On 21 and 22 November some boys from the school went on strike in support of their teacher and marched through Penparcau and the town centre chanting, 'The governors ought to be shot, shot, shot.'

In a further meeting in December the governors decided to rescind the previous decision, but only by means of the casting vote of the chairman, the Revd R J Rees. This decision was welcomed by the Editor of *The Cambrian News*, who wrote: 'Our young men are sent out to exterminate Prussianism abroad; and are we going to allow a kindred spirit to rear its head in our midst at home?'

Davies remained a teacher at the County School until 1930, when he was dismissed, allegedly by a vengeful Headmaster who had served in the war.

Another teacher who went before the Cardigan Rural Tribunal in 1916 claiming to be a conscientious objector was T Bryn Jones, who was at that time the Headmaster of Aberporth Council School. His application for absolute exemption at the Tribunal was rejected but his appeal to the County Tribunal was accompanied by a letter stating:

> I have a serious objection to taking life and I have been preaching that for the last ten years. I believe that international disputes could be settled without the shedding of blood. However, I am patriotic and I should like to do something short of taking life for my country. I understand mine sweeping is dangerous and that men are wanted in that sphere.

Unlike Davies, who was an absolutist (that is, he was unwilling to serve in any capacity relating to warfare), Jones was therefore prepared to undertake any duties as long as he was not expected to bear arms.

The decision of the Local Tribunal, 'exemption from Combatant service only. Not indispensable' was upheld by the County Tribunal. As a result, Jones served for the last two years of the war with a Non-Combatant Corps (NCC) in France, undertaking manual tasks such as moving timber and stones. Members of the NCC were subject to the Army's organisation and discipline except that they did not bear arms. They were often referred to as the 'No Courage Corps'.

On his return, Jones was told by a local councillor, Captain B T Davies of Aberporth, who had been a recruiting agent during the war, that he would not be considered for a post back in his old school. By the spring of 1919 he had found employment at Tregroes School near Llandysul, but soon after applied for the post of Headmaster of Cribyn School near Lampeter. Although selected by the appointments panel, many of the parents objected – partly because of his pacifist beliefs. The parents kept their children at home from school in protest. The matter was raised in the county's Education Committee and once more C M Williams, the persecutor of D J Davies, was prominent in his criticism of the proposed appointment. There was a public spat between Williams and Councillor John Gibson, who had been critical of Williams in the past.

In the event, the Education Committee refused to ratify the appointment and T Bryn Jones returned to Tregroes School. However, when the headmastership of that school became vacant in September 1919, parents and local councillors were anxious to appoint Jones. Nevertheless, the education authority appointed another candidate, Ben James. The angry parents, who had supported T Bryn Jones, kept their children home from school and on his first day in November 1919, the new head wrote simply in the school log book: 'No children present'. The strike lasted until January 1920, when a compromise was reached. The Education Authority agreed that were the headmastership of Tregroes to become vacant in the future, Jones would be appointed. It is clear that an understanding had been reached with Ben James, who a few weeks later was appointed Headmaster of Pontsian School. He was replaced by T Bryn Jones, who remained as Headmaster at Tregroes until his retirement in 1951.

*

When the armistice was announced on 11 November 1918, press reports suggested that it was children who inspired the rejoicing. In Llandysul the children shouted themselves hoarse, while in Aberystwyth, whereas adults felt mixed emotions relating to the:

> ...hardship, the sorrow, and, above all, the soul-eating anxiety... the children, as usual, showed the way... bands of boys paraded the streets, drumming on every conceivable thing that would make noise. Blasts of horns came from one direction, the crash of detonators from another. It was an occasion for noise after years of silence.

It was also said of the children that 'they knew not the sorrow, but they realised the occasion to rejoice.' Nevertheless, children had also experienced dislocation, hardship and grief during a war which cut across their young lives. They were indocrinated with patriotic beliefs which centred on the perceived greatness of the British Empire and the sacrifices made by young men to defend it. For many, such a viewpoint would remain with them for the remainder of their lives but, in time, others would come to a very different conclusion.

Two Irreconcilables: T E Nicholas and John Fitzwilliams

I love Hun shooting; it is much more fun than bunnies.

LETTER TO HIS WIFE FROM JOHN FITZWILLIAMS, 1915

I am writing to ask you if you can do anything to help to get a most objectionable and dangerous man in this neighbourhood put away for a bit. He is a chapel minister in our village of Llangybi.

LETTER FROM WINIFRED INGLIS-JONES, 1917

THE EFFECT OF the Russian Revolution of 1917 on Ceredigion was minimal but its impact on two men who lived a good part of their lives in the county was immeasurable.

The Revd T E Nicholas and Major John Fitzwilliams were born no more than ten miles apart from one another. During the First World War, the home of Fitzwilliams's family was about 25 miles from Nicholas's home near Lampeter, but they were unlikely to have ever met. Indeed, despite the relatively close proximity of their respective residences in the Teifi Valley, their backgrounds and attitude towards the war could not have been more different.

T E Nicholas

John Fitzwilliams

T E Nicholas had settled as a chapel minister in Llangybi near Lampeter in January 1914, by which time John Fitzwilliams was already building a career as a lieutenant with the Royal Horse Artillery. The latter's family home was Cilgwyn, Adpar, on the Ceredigion side of the River Teifi, where he was born in 1884. Nicholas had been born five years earlier in the village of Llanfyrnach on the Pembrokeshire side of the Teifi.

There were major differences in their upbringing. Fitzwilliams came from a comfortably rich minor gentry family, while Nicholas's father was a humble smallholder and stonemason. Nicholas was a Welsh speaker but Fitzwilliams, though living as a child in a Welsh-speaking community where several of his near neighbours were monoglot Welsh, was monolingual, speaking only English. Later he learnt some Russian and German, but never Welsh. The Fitzwilliamses were churchgoers, whereas Nicholas attended the local Independent chapel with his mother.

Their backgrounds were therefore entirely different, both materially and culturally, but they both held firm beliefs on their calling, as exemplified by Nicholas's letters to the press, his poems and his newspaper columns during the war, and by Fitzwilliams's surviving letters from the front, mainly to his wife Margery.

*

John Kendrick Lloyd Fitzwilliams was one of five brothers who served with the armed forces during the First World War. He was the youngest of the ten children of Charles Home Lloyd Fitzwilliams and his wife Margaret Alicia, Cilgwyn. He was educated at Christ College Brecon and at Dover College, before passing into the Royal Military Academy, Woolwich (now Sandhurst) in 1902. In 1904 he joined the 139th Battery of the Royal Horse Artillery, subsequently spending some time in Moscow and Berlin on language interpreterships.

He married Margery Laura Hyde in 1910 and the following year was promoted to G Battery of the Royal Horse Artillery, famed for its exploits at the Battle of Waterloo a hundred years earlier. During the first weeks of the war, G Battery undertook an intensive period of training in Ipswich prior to embarking for France in November 1914.

By this time the war had settled into a long period of stalemate, interspersed with vicious and mostly futile battles. The young lieutenant (he was later promoted captain and then major) expressed his hatred for the Germans in a number of letters home. 'They are pigs, aren't they?', he wrote. 'It gives me infinite joy to shoot at Germans,' he exclaimed in March 1915 and, later in the year, 'I love Hun shooting; it is much more fun than bunnies.'

On his wife's birthday, 12 May 1915, he reported that he had killed a German: 'I wish you would have a birthday every day of the year. I send him to you with my best love as a birthday present. I know you will value it more than anything else I can give you.'

The following day he wrote: 'The Germans bombed one of our trenches today and one fellow put his ugly head over the parapet, upon which a timid Terrier jabbed his bayonet into his throat and pulled the trigger, with the result that he got a complete German's head as a souvenir and is very proud of himself.'

Later in the war he was to write: 'I went round to the Infantry General who is young and energetic and is absorbed with the one and sole idea of killing Huns... This morning there were twenty-two nice fat Huns, quite dead, lying outside their barbed wire.'

Fitzwilliams's views were not always insensitive: he showed sympathy for the ordinary soldier living in 'filthy and evil-smelling' trenches, and on the Somme in 1916 he surveyed a battlefield where 'The sight of the wounded made me want to cry from sheer inability to help them. It was just awful.'

Nevertheless, in general, his views were typical of the public school-educated officer class, who were utterly confident that their cause was just and considered it their duty to defend 'King and country'. This would be achieved by killing as many of the enemy as possible. These would not have been T E Nicholas's views and he would have been horrified had he read the comments in Fitzwilliams's letters.

*

Following a happy if impoverished childhood in a culturally enriched Welsh-speaking rural community, Nicholas moved to south Wales as a young man. He was ordained in 1901, becoming an Independent minister at Llandeilo, then briefly in Dodgeville, Wisconsin, and most famously at Glais in the Swansea Valley. From this point on, he became known as 'Niclas y Glais'. During this period he became a socialist, joining the Independent Labour Party (ILP) in 1905, and was well-known for his fiery sermons based on a radical interpretation of the Gospels and an emphasis on social justice for working people. He married Mary Alys Hopkins in 1904 and had three children with her, but he appears not always to have complied with the seventh commandment. In 1914 he became Minister of Ebeneser Chapel at Llangybi near Lampeter and Bethlehem in Llanddewi Brefi.

Nicholas served as the first Welsh-language editor of the ILP's newspaper, *The Merthyr Pioneer*, from its foundation in 1911 and from August 1914 onwards he contributed a series of articles to it, opposing the war. These articles were in Welsh and were often followed by a poem castigating those whom he considered responsible for the war.

To him, there had never been such a thing as a just war and there never would be. He claimed that a nation could not do what was forbidden to an individual: if it is unjust for an individual to kill his enemy then the same must also apply to nations. He also warned that it was the stronger nation who would win the war, not necessarily the one which was deemed to be in the right.

He was persistent in his attacks on the Nonconformist denominations which supported the war and the ministers who encouraged young members of their chapels to join the armed forces. He waspishly pointed out that these denominations persistently complained to the Government that small shops selling sweets were open on Sundays while never drawing attention to all the killing that took place on the Sabbath on the continent.

He was also critical of some leaders of the Labour movement for failing to oppose the war. He claimed peace should be the aim of Labour and religion; neither could gain anything from the shedding of blood. He had no sympathy for the Kaiser or German militarism but pointed to the atrocities committed by the Belgians in the Congo and to Britain's ally, the Russian Tsar, whose treatment of his people was unequivocally tyrannical.

*

While Fitzwilliams was in the midst of the fighting, Nicholas was also active, as the county's organiser for the No-Conscription Fellowship, opposing the Military Service Act which had introduced conscription in 1916. Nicholas was known to assist those in the county wishing to register as conscientious objectors, often by filling in forms on their behalf.

He continued to preach and lecture in south Wales, often on platforms with pacifists. He was to stand for Parliament for the Aberdare seat in the General Election held after the war ended in 1918 but, despite his popularity in some quarters, he was heavily defeated by the pro-war candidate C B Stanton.

Nicholas was also instrumental in establishing branches of the farm workers' union NALRU in the county, speaking in over 20 meetings in north Pembrokeshire and Ceredigion during the latter years of the war. He also sought support specifically from lead miners. In a meeting held in Pontrhydygroes in early December 1917, it was reported that Nicholas:

> ...laid stress on the importance of forming a union. He showed how workmen who had not united in the past were suffering, and how those who had united were reaping the fruits of their labour to-day. The salvation of the working man lies in his joining a union.

These activities made him unpopular among landowners and businessmen anxious to retain their ability to control wages and working conditions.

According to one local dignitary, Nicholas preached sedition from the pulpit. Mrs Winifred Inglis-Jones resided at Derry Ormond, a mansion near to the chapel where Nicholas was the Minister. By coincidence, she served on the Ceredigion committee of the Soldiers' and Sailors' Families Association alongside John Fitzwilliams's mother, and perhaps this is the only verifiable – though tenuous – link between the two men.

In November 1917, Mrs Inglis-Jones wrote to Mrs Flora Drummond, a formidable leading figure in the pro-war Women's Party:

> Dear Mrs Drummond
>
> I am writing to ask you if you can do anything to help to get a most objectionable and dangerous man in this neighbourhood put away for a bit. He is a chapel minister in our village of Llangybi...
>
> When you stayed with us in 1915, I spoke to you and Colonel Hunter about him. He was then openly preaching sedition in his chapel and abusing our King and doing all in his power to stop recruiting.
>
> I know that Colonel Hunter said that he had been warned and was being watched. For two years this Nicholas has been quiet in these parts but he has been all over this country preaching at other places. Now he is getting very bad again. He has taken up the cause of the conscientious objector. What he says causes great

annoyance to the better thinking portion of his congregation, but it is doing untold harm to others, especially to the young who of course go to hear anything so dareing [sic] and original as his utterances. The difficulty to me is that it is all in Welsh and I can get no real record of his sermon. But I can assure you that it all much encourages the pacifist and pro-German propoganda [sic] and if this Nicholas could be made an example of it would go a long way towards restoring a patriotic feeling...

There were attempts to prosecute Nicholas but the authorities were anxious to avoid creating a martyr. When he did come before the magistrates at Lampeter in June 1918, accused of uttering a statement likely to cause disaffection amongst the civil population, the case was dropped.

In 1917, Nicholas welcomed the revolution in Russia which saw the Tsar overthrown and ultimately led to the victory of the Bolsheviks later in the year. But while Nicholas viewed these events from afar, Fitzwilliams had first-hand experience of the situation in Russia during that most turbulent of periods.

*

Fitzwilliams had been wounded in the spring of 1917 and, whilst convalescing in England, was called to join up with Colonel Terence Keyes on a propaganda mission to Russia. They were both chosen because of their knowledge of the Russian language. There were grave concerns in the British Government that the Russians, following the February revolution, might bring their involvement in the war to an end. This would mean that the German Army in eastern Europe could be transferred to the Western Front and tip the balance of the fighting in Germany's favour. Fitzwilliams and Keyes were appointed 'King's Messengers' and sent to Russia and its neighbouring countries to persuade them to continue to fight.

The mission began in Petrograd (St Petersburg) in July 1917, and they then travelled to the Ukraine and subsequently on to Romania, which remained a strategically important, if weak, supporter of the Allies. In Romania, Fitzwilliams spent some time with the Romanian royal family (based in what is now Moldova), including Queen Marie, Queen Victoria's granddaughter, and her daughter Princess Elizabeth. Propaganda films were shown to the Russian troops defending Romania in the hope that they would not turn mutinous, as had been the case elsewhere.

In October 1917, the Bolsheviks captured Petrograd and went on to extend their control to other parts of the Russian Empire. In December, Fitzwilliams was dispatched from Romania to Kiev, the capital of the Ukraine, with the task of encouraging the famous Don Cossacks and others to resist the Bolshevik advance and to report to the British Government on the fraught situation in that country. He carried with him eight bills of £5,000 each of British Government money, as well as the authority to provide £10 million more to aid the resistance.

However, when the mission failed and the Bolsheviks took control of the Ukrainian Government in Kiev in January 1918, the British Government feared that food and materials could fall into German hands, as the Germans were advancing into the Ukraine. Consequently Fitzwilliams set about distributing to the general population food supplies purchased by the British and stored in Kiev for use by the anti-Bolshevik forces, as well as destroying motor tyres, which would have been valuable to an advancing army.

In February Fitzwilliams and others at the British Mission in Kiev left the city by the Trans-Siberian Railway, heading for Vladivostok in the extreme east of the country, as travelling west through enemy territory was impossible. Among those also on the train was Tomáš Masaryk, subsequently to become the first President of Czechoslovakia.

Fitzwilliams returned to Britain via the United States and by August 1918 was back in France, commanding Z Battery of the 126th Army Brigade. On 30 August, a shell exploded near him and he was killed instantly. Had he survived, he would no doubt have returned to Russia after the war to fight against the Bolsheviks in the Russian Civil War, in which the British backed the 'White Russians' who opposed the 'Red' Communists.

There was no doubting where Nicholas's sympathies lay in the bloody and uncompromising civil war in Russia. Although he has often been described as a pacifist, he had no qualms about supporting the violent methods of the Bolsheviks in gaining power. By 1920 he had joined the fledgling British Communist Party. He was to remain a member over the ensuing fifty years of his life and was famed for his defence of Stalin, despite the latter's tyrannical rule. Although he continued to preach, Nicholas left the ministry in 1918 and henceforth earned his living as a less-than-skilful dentist in Aberystwyth. To some on the left he cut a heroic figure, who stood up to the political and religious establishment of his day, but in truth he was no more than an eccentric – if attractive – voice who had little lasting influence.

Nicholas and Fitzwilliams possessed completely contrary perspectives, yet were similar in many ways. They were both confident in their beliefs and uncompromisingly belligerent in expressing them. Fitzwilliams died with victory for his cause in sight but those objectives of social justice and peace espoused by Nicholas have remained elusive.

The Soldier's Return

*The British Empire is & will remain the
greatest community of men for the good of mankind.*
PRIVATE BILL JONES, ABERYSTWYTH

Four years of hateful fighting and little to show for it.
PRIVATE JOHN DAVIES, LAMPETER

RATHER TACTLESSLY, THE townspeople of Aberystwyth were
alerted that the war had come to an end on 11 November
1918 by the firing of a lifeboat's gun on the Promenade; as if
not enough guns had been fired over the previous four years.
Elsewhere church and school bells were rung, while the GWR
train to Carmarthen, as it passed through the county's villages,
hooted loudly to signify the end of hostilities. In Aberaeron, a
large bonfire was lit on a hill above the town.

There was widespread rejoicing in Aberystwyth, with
flags and bunting on display and children marching through
the streets of the town '...drumming on every conceivable
thing that would make a noise'. Meanwhile in Aberaeron
'...a procession of flare bearers paraded the town, headed by a
band of promiscuous instruments and a drum'. Lampeter was
decorated with flags and bunting and it was reported that a
'somewhat curious feature in connection with the decorations
was that the work was done by German prisoners, and that,

apparently, with relish and gusto'. They too were clearly pleased, anticipating a return to their homeland.

Nevertheless, the rejoicing was tinged with relief. *The Cambrian News* reported:

> The hardship, the sorrow, and, above all, the soul-eating anxiety. All over. People could hardly believe it, and were hesitant to rejoice. The sorrows of four years could not be thrown aside in a minute.

The response in some rural villages was muted. In Swyddffynnon, it was reported:

> A few quiet tears were shed by the relatives of the fallen who will return no more, but no cheering, no conflagrations, and no flag waving broke the wonted calm of the village.

In Pontrhydfendigaid '...the public evinced suppressed joy... Thanksgiving services at the places of worship marked the long-wished-for event.' At Cwrtnewydd School a 'peace oak' was planted in the playground.

The peace celebrations in Cardigan, July 1919
(courtesy of Archifdy Ceredigion Archives)

It was not until July 1919, following the signing of the Treaty of Versailles, that widespread official celebrations took place throughout the country. By then most of the soldiers and sailors had returned home in dribs and drabs over a period of several months.

*

Among the first to return were the prisoners of war, including some civilians who had been interned in 1914 at Ruhleben Camp in Berlin, where a total of about 5,000 men had been incarcerated. David Evans, originally from Blaenffos near Cardigan, was a lecturer in Charlottenburg, Germany before the war. He was interned at Ruhleben in October 1914 and spent much of his time at the camp teaching his fellow inmates, becoming the camp's head of Celtic studies. On his return, he became a lecturer at Aberystwyth College, where he was known affectionately by the students as 'Dai Deutsch'. At the camp he had lectured with a brilliant young Cambridge graduate, Ivor Leslie Evans. Evans, originally from Aberdare, learnt Welsh at the camp and was soon lecturing to his fellow-inmates on Welsh poetry. He changed his name to Ifor L Evans and in 1934 came to Aberystwyth as one of the College's more distinguished Principals.

Many of the prisoners of war had been captured during the German advance in the spring of 1918. They returned home with tales of ill-treatment and starvation. Among these was Dai Sayce from Cardigan, who had fought at Mons, Loos and Cambrai. In March 1918 he had tried to escape a German attack but was shot in the back. He was ill-treated by some drunken German soldiers but was aided by a more compassionate enemy soldier. He was eventually treated by fellow soldiers at a camp for the wounded near Mons, and after recovering, he was imprisoned at Marburg, spending the rest of the war working on local farms. In a ceremony welcoming him home to Cardigan, he presented the town's Mayoress with a piece of black rye bread, a day's ration for a prisoner of war in Germany.

Despite the harsh conditions in the camps, it was the lack of food which most distressed the prisoners. Another son of Cardigan, Lieutenant Leonard V D Owen, who spent 20 months in prisoner of war camps in Germany, reported that many prisoners would have died had they not received the Red Cross parcels sent from home:

> The treatment of the men, especially the British, was marked by callous neglect of the most elementary principles of humanity. Bullied, starved, and overworked and even forced to work immediately behind the German front line, hundreds died, or, saved by the armistice, were returned in a condition of appalling neglect.
>
> We found a trainload of British prisoners at Worms Station [in the Rhineland] who were in the last stages of starvation, clothed in rags, and many wearing wooden clogs on their stockingless feet. Most of these unfortunate men were survivors of gangs who had been forced to work behind the German lines defending Metz, and had died by scores from starvation, disease, and the Allied shell fire.

Owen also remarked that there was widespread starvation among the German people, particularly the poor. This was a consequence of the economic blockades which undermined the capacity of the Germans to wage war and keep their population fed and healthy. It is little wonder then that the prisoners of war were at the extreme lower end of the pecking order.

*

It took several months for soldiers, sailors and airmen to demobilise. Some stayed in the Rhineland, Germany, as an occupying force. The press reported in January 1919 that six soldiers from Penparcau had been discharged or were home on leave, but another, Private J D Hughes, Rheidol View, was in Cologne. He had written home from the German city:

> We arrived in the city about three weeks ago, the residents gazing through their windows as we paraded the streets. We are billeted in one of the finest barracks ever built and are allowed to visit the Cathedral and other public buildings.

No doubt Cologne Cathedral was a more imposing place of worship than Ebeneser Chapel, '*y capel bach*' which he attended at home.

Other Aberystwyth soldiers were much further afield that month. Private George E Hammond wrote home from Damascus, Syria, while Private T J Delahay of North Parade was with the North Russian Expeditionary Force at Murmansk in the freezing north of Russia, fighting with the 'White Russians' against the Bolsheviks. Private J M Michell was in Bombay (now Mumbai), India.

A great number of meetings were held throughout the county to welcome home the soldiers. A 'hearty reception concert' was arranged in Penbryn near Cardigan in August 1919 to welcome home Private Jacob Griffiths. In Pontrhydfendigaid:

> [a] Cordial reception was given Lance Corpl. W. Jones-Edwards; Ptes. Edward Morgan, John Herbert, John Ebenezer, Percy Morgan, and Daniel Rhys Jones... The singing and recitations were of a high order and a crowded audience gave the lads a really hearty welcome. The Chairman delivered an address and the Conductor presented the usual gift to each soldier.

However, some soldiers did not welcome such attention. A large crowd and a band gathered at Cardigan station in November 1918 to greet Gunner Arthur Evans, who had been a prisoner of war. Having seen the crowd, Evans jumped off the train on the wrong side and slipped away unnoticed through the Mercantile Yard.

Some soldiers returned home with wives. Alf Jenkins of Tygof, Ponterwyd, who had served with the Royal Army Medical Corps, had married an Irish nurse who had worked at the same hospital as him. When, after demobilisation, he brought her home with their newborn son, his mother refused to allow her into the house. The couple subsequently lived apart but they remained married and he would visit her and his son in England on a regular basis until his death in 1982.

Lance Corporal D J Evans MM was an Aberystwyth veteran of campaigns in China, Gallipoli, Egypt and France, where he was awarded the Military Medal in 1916 while serving with the Royal Welsh Fusiliers (having previously been with the South Wales Borderers). On 8 January 1918 he married a Belgian woman, Alice Pype, in Neuville-des-Dieppe, but was soon after captured during the German offensive of March 1918 and spent the remainder of the war as a prisoner working in coal mines in Germany. His wife meanwhile gave birth, but the child died after two weeks. On his return to Aberystwyth with his wife, 'Dai MM', as he became known, worked as a postman in Aberystwyth.

*

Some of those who survived the fighting were to succumb to the deadly 'Spanish flu' influenza pandemic which had spread throughout the world, killing over fifty million people worldwide – several times more than those killed in battle.

Gunner Dick Millman of Trefechan died of influenza in France in December 1918, having survived over four years in the Army. Likewise Private Lemuel Tom Rees of Blaenannerch died in Boulogne of bronchial pneumonia following influenza, only two days after the armistice had been signed. Private David Matthew Williams of Cardigan had served with the Royal Welsh Fusiliers and the Durham Light Infantry in France since 1917, but he too fell ill soon after the armistice. He died in a hospital in England and his body was brought home for burial locally in March 1919. He was 19 years old.

Many who returned suffered both mentally and physically. Arthur S Mathias of Cardigan, who had enlisted with the Royal Engineers in 1915, was an inmate of Brecon Asylum when he died in April 1919 aged 35. He was probably a victim of shell shock, or as it would be termed today, post-traumatic stress disorder. Private Evan J Jones of Aberbanc, Llandysul, lost an eye in the fighting, but was able to find employment as a postman in the Henllan and Bryngwenith area. Richard Jones of Llangwyryfon had been discharged with gunshot wounds to the hip and hand, while W L Jones of Ponterwyd suffered from 'trench nephritis', which was characterised by breathlessness, swelling of the face or legs, headache, and sore throat. Others suffered from 'trench foot', caused by prolonged exposure to the damp, unsanitary and icy conditions experienced in the trenches. Yet others suffered from deafness, tuberculosis or lung damage caused by poison gas.

Mustard gas had many pernicious side-effects. David John Jones from Aberystwyth served as a signaller on the Western Front in France with the Royal Field Artillery. He fell victim to mustard gas at Ypres in the spring of 1918. He was unable to speak for over a year – however, in May 1919, he attended a football match at Blackpool and when a goal was scored, he excitedly shouted, "Goal!" To his surprise, his powers of speech had returned.

All these casualties were entitled to varying amounts of pension, administered by local War Pensions Committees. There were different classifications, according to the severity of the disability. Private Johnny Davies of Pren-gwyn, Llandysul, who was blinded during the Gallipoli campaign, would have received a full pension but John B Edwards of Llanafan, who had his right arm amputated, would have received only 50% of the full pension, despite his incapacity. It was reported that by the end of July 1919 there were 1,059 discharged and demobilised ex-servicemen recorded on the county's War Pensions Committee's register. Of the 53 who had been added to the register in July, 9 received inpatient treatment, 36 outpatient treatment, 39 home treatment, and 5 cases were awaiting treatment in orthopaedic hospitals. Many considered the pensions awarded inadequate to live on. The Government was reluctant to apportion funds to adequately recompense those who had fought for King and country and relied to a large extent on philanthropic and charitable contributions administered by local voluntary organisations.

Some of those injured in battle died during the years after the war. David Rowland Jones of Dolfawr, Tregaron, had been wounded in France during the war. He had returned home, only for his health to deteriorate as a result of his wounds. He died aged 32 in September 1919. However, Willie Evans, Hafod, Nantcwnlle, only succumbed to the injuries he had suffered in the war in February 1930.

Many ex-servicemen returned to their previous occupations and this sometimes entailed the female staff who had undertaken this work during the war being dismissed. Although this was understandable at the time, women felt that the increasingly important roles that they had played at a time of crisis were now all too easily discarded. Women over the age of 30 had been given the vote by the Parliament (Qualification of Women) Act 1918 and they expected wider recognition of their contribution to society. The Llanilar Debating Society, always a source of progressive social discussion, held a debate in December 1918 on the proposal that 'Women should receive equal pay with men for equal work.' The proposer was Miss Jane Richards who lived at Meillionen, Llanilar, but as she was absent, Mr J J Jones took her place. Two women and one other man spoke in favour, while four men opposed. A vote was taken and the resolution was passed by twenty votes to ten. The women of Llanilar, as elsewhere, are still waiting for this proposal to come to full fruition over a hundred years later.

*

The number of students studying at Aberystwyth College increased substantially after the war, with 971 registered students in October 1919 as compared to 429 in the year before the war. The number of staff also increased and buildings on the Promenade were renovated to provide student accommodation. As early as November 1917, provision had been made for a two-year elementary teacher-training course for disabled discharged soldiers, and most of the post-war students were ex-servicemen.

Over a hundred students, either enrolled at the College in 1914 or alumni, had been killed during the war and it is not surprising that there was a bitter attitude by returning soldiers towards the conscientious objectors who had refused to fight. When the College's Graduation Ceremony was held at the National Library of Wales in 1919, a raucous gang of students were in the audience. When a well-known conscientious objector, William James Lewis, walked to the stage to receive his degree, he was greeted with derision by the students. The incident was later described in vivid detail by H M Vaughan, who was present at the ceremony. He wrote:

> ...on the further side of the room a group of young College students, who had served and fought in the war recently ended, had settled themselves as an impromptu band armed with a number of musical instruments of torture such as tin trumpets, mouth-organs and the like. Squatting on the floor these ex-service men gave vent from the time to time to expressions of approval or disapproval during the ceremony of granting degrees. Amongst those standing ready in academic robes to receive the degree of bachelor, I soon noticed our friend, the tall red-haired Shropshire "Conchie"; and as he advanced towards the Pro-Chancellor, Lord Kenyon, the watchful band of youngsters on the floor set up a fearful howling and started to play their musical instruments with redoubled vigour. There were loud shouts of "Yah, yah. Conchie! Successful Shirker! Conscientious Objectors get first-class

honours!" etc etc. Not a word of Lord Kenyon's remarks could be heard above the din whilst he was capping this unpopular fellow-student. After receiving his degree from the Pro-Chancellor, the Shropshire lad had to walk down the further side of the room and thus pass close to the noisy coterie on the floor. As he approached them the ex-servicemen pelted him with missiles, which were wrongly but perhaps charitably described in the local newspapers as "balls of brown paper," but were in reality raw potatoes, for one of these ill-aimed objects happened to hit me in the back and I picked it up from the floor. The newly-created Bachelor of the University of Wales certainly had to run the gauntlet of reproof and derision, to say nothing of the raw potatoes, before he could reach a place of quiet and safety.

The attitude among some students towards conscientious objectors was to change in due course. In December 1923 the most prominent and outspoken Welsh conscientious objector during the war, George Maitland Lloyd Davies, was elected Member of Parliament for the University of Wales constituency. The electorate for this seat, a peculiarity of the time, was made up of graduates of the four constituent colleges of the University of Wales, including Aberystwyth. Of the 36% of the voters who supported Davies, there must have been many from Aberystwyth and they may even have included some of those bitter ex-servicemen of 1919.

*

Many ex-servicemen joined local branches of the Comrades of the Great War, an organisation which sought to represent the interests of ex-soldiers and their dependants – particularly those in need. The county's honorary secretary, F S Trufant of Aberarth, wrote a column in *The Cambrian News* entitled 'Comrades Column', in which he reported on the members' grievances and the efforts being made at a local and national level to improve their lot. In June 1919, he reported that the Comrades were seeking to raise the gratuity paid to each ex-soldier to £50 for each year of service and, in a meeting in Aberaeron, it was claimed that the results of individual local cases taken up by the Comrades had proved satisfactory. However, in his column in December 1919, Trufant complained about the growth of battlefield tourism, with photographs being taken of smiling visitors '"seeing the sights" where death and desolation reigned but a short year ago'. He continued:

> During the war we were hard put to it to find words strong enough to express our opinions of conchies, p[r]ofiteers, and the like; but the worst of these misfits were more human than those who would seek more profit or sensations over the graves of our glorious dead.

The Comrades and other similar organisations such as the National Association of Discharged Sailors and Soldiers, also active in the county, eventually amalgamated in 1921 and the British Legion was formed. The Aberystwyth branch committee of the British Legion included veterans of the war such as the chemist, Captain Bertie Taylor-Lloyd MC, the schoolmaster, W George Rowlands (who had been severely gassed) and the postman, D J Evans MM.

Those involved with the British Legion and who paraded on Remembrance Sunday tended to take great satisfaction in their achievements and those of their comrades, both dead and alive. This was coupled with a militaristic spirit, saturated in Britishness, which tended to eclipse their Welsh identity. They also carried with them the values and beliefs of comradeship which they had previously described in letters home during the war. Private David Rowlands of Aberystwyth, for example, had written home from France in 1915 referring to 'what a great big family we are out here', while Private Bill Jones of Plas Crug, Aberystwyth, wrote from the Suez Canal Zone in July 1916 that he and his comrades believed that those who sought to avoid conscription at the Military Service Tribunals '...ought to be shot as traitors to liberty... The British Empire is & will remain the greatest community of men for the good of mankind.' On their return, the experiences of ex-servicemen would be a great source of storytelling over a pint of beer and indeed brought colour to lives which could henceforward often be drab and uneventful.

Some ex-servicemen became bitter because the 'land fit for heroes' which they had been given to expect on their return turned out to be far from the truth. During the 1920s and 1930s there was an economic downturn, and an agricultural depression which was particularly damaging for rural communities. The woollen mills of the Teifi Valley, which had experienced a brief boom during the war, closed down, and there was widespread unemployment throughout the county. It appeared to some ex-servicemen that their sacrifices had been in vain and, during strikes and protests throughout Britain, placards were displayed with unequivocal messages such as 'The Unemployed Ex-Servicemen demand work not "doles"' and 'the dead are remembered but we are forgotten'.

Other ex-servicemen refused to talk about their experiences, in an attempt to erase from their memories the most horrendous ordeal of their lives. John Jones of Dihewyd, who served with the Welsh Guards, lost a brother in the war but was reluctant to speak of his own experiences. When he did so, it was tinged with the guilt that he had survived, while a comrade had not, when a bomb exploded in a dugout where they were sheltering. On being transferred to a field hospital, John Jones was elated that he had received a 'Blighty wound' which meant that he might now be sent home, but he regretted that he had failed to express any concern about the fate of the other soldier. Such feelings of self-reproach haunted him for the rest of his life. He also had physical evidence of his own ordeal, as he took to his grave the piece of shrapnel which remained buried in his arm. He did not attend chapel after the war, as he was disillusioned by the attitude of ministers who had, from the pulpit, urged young men to enlist.

*

There was a strong desire among the civilian population, as well as the returning servicemen, to commemorate those who had died on the battlefield. Committees were established in all communities and funds raised to create fitting memorials, although these came in differing forms. Some communities sought to create permanent physical memorials in prominent positions in the centre of villages or towns, where relatives of the dead could grieve and the general public could gather on Armistice Day to pay their respects.

The memorials listed the names of casualties but took different styles. In the south of the county, and in particular in the Teifi Valley, the memorials tended to be statues of soldiers in various poses, standing on a pedestal. The bronze statue at Lampeter was particularly impressive, as it was sculpted by the famous Welsh artist and sculptor W Goscombe John. To the north there were at least half a dozen memorials in the form of a large Celtic cross. There appears to be only one of these in a community in the south of the county, at Neuadd Cross near Llandygwydd. Other memorials were either a cenotaph or an obelisk. The most unusual memorial in the county is perhaps that at Pontrhydfendigaid: a white marble female figure representing peace, standing on a red granite pedestal. The most spectacular memorial, however, was that located on the promontory on the site of Aberystwyth Castle. Designed by an Italian sculptor, Mario Rutelli, the memorial – which is nearly 20 metres high – is crowned by winged Victory standing on a globe. It was unveiled on 14 September 1923 and includes the names of 111 servicemen from Aberystwyth who lost their lives during the war.

Other communities sought to commemorate the dead in, many would claim, a more useful way. They raised funds to build a *neuadd goffa* ['memorial hall'] which would be a valuable long-term community resource. These *neuaddau*

A Celtic cross: the Llanafan war memorial

(author's own photograph)

The Pontrhydfendigaid war memorial

(courtesy of Iestyn Hughes)

coffa remain vital centres in villages and small towns such as Llanrhystud, Sarnau, Capel Bangor, Tregaron and Aberaeron. Most contain plaques listing those killed in the war and some, such as Neuadd Goffa Tal-y-bont, also record the names of those who served but survived.

A similar mindset was prevalent in Cardigan, where a substantial residence called The Priory – designed by the architect John Nash, famous for Brighton's Royal Pavilion and Buckingham Palace – was converted into the Cardigan and District Memorial Hospital, which was opened in 1922. Nevertheless, some townspeople remained anxious to commemorate the dead by creating a permanent memorial in the town. Eventually, a large cenotaph was placed in Victoria Gardens, near the centre of Cardigan, which bore the names of the 91 servicemen from the district who had died in the war. The names of those who were killed in the Second World War were, in due course, added to this and to other memorials across the county.

Despite the public memorials, the personal grief of families at the loss of a father, husband or brother would remain constant, and some never recovered. The family of Private David Samuel Roberts, killed in September 1918, would always refer to his former home, Soar, Cilcennin, as '*tŷ galar*' ['house of sorrow'].

*

Some communities published booklets as a means of recording the service and sacrifice of local men and women. They were often shrouded in sadness but occasionally forthright in their opinions, such as in the introduction to the book of remembrance for the war dead of Cribyn, near Lampeter. Here is a translation from Welsh of the anonymous author's views in 1922:

As in other parts of the country, the Cribyn area raised men capable of answering great summonses at an important hour. From homes in the neighbourhood, boys went out to face the enemy in the field and at sea. They were never captivated by military pomp, and insignificant in their view were the traditions of militarism. They went out to fight for principle as much as for country. Their objective was not to depose militarism in one country and to install it in another. Instead they faced the horrors of war to establish peace on earth and freedom for the weak to live. To fully appreciate their service, the erection of a handsome monument is not enough to keep their remembrance alive: one must fight until the principle for which so many were sacrificed is respected throughout the world. Is it possible that the strong among us are violating the weak and the defenceless are suffering, not under a foreign heel? The price of freedom is eternal vigilance.

There were also memoirs. J M Davies of Ponterwyd published his memoirs in Welsh in 1966. *O Gwmpas Pumlumon: Atgofion a Hanesion* ['Around Pumlumon: Recollections and Anecdotes'] gives an entertaining account of his experiences with the South Wales Borderers. He was among those who fought at Pilkem Ridge on 31 July 1917, the battle in which the poet Hedd Wyn was killed. Davies took great pride in the achievements of the Welsh soldiers that day and wrote *'Rown ni yno, ac yn falch o hynny'* ['I was there, and am proud of it']. William Jones-Edwards was also at Pilkem Ridge but his memoir, *Ar Lethrau Ffair Rhos* ['On the Slopes of Ffair Rhos'], published in 1963, is rather more tinged with sadness.

In later interviews, some ex-soldiers were adamant that the war had been a wasteful exercise. John Davies from the Lampeter area was one:

> ...the war was a total waste. What was it to me? And how much better are we today? Four years of hateful fighting and little to show for it. I don't see the point of it at all. [translation]

*

The Great War was a devastating industrialised war on a massive scale, in which more than ten million people died. It was not a 'necessary war', as some would claim, and it was certainly not 'a just war', a much-quoted oxymoron. The historian Margaret Macmillan has written:

> If we want to point fingers from the twenty-first century, we can accuse those who took Europe into war of two things. First, a failure of imagination in not seeing how destructive such a conflict would be and second, their lack of courage to stand up to those who said there was no choice left but to go [to] war. There are always choices.

The war was caused by the aggressive greed and ambitions of the Great Powers of Europe, anxious to expand or protect their exploitative empires. The monarchs (who were mostly related to each other) and the political establishments of these countries had placed their own interests before those of their people. And it was the people who suffered, including those of Ceredigion.

Aberystwyth Borough Councillors and Officials, Peace Celebrations July 1919 (courtesy of Archifdy Ceredigion Archives)

Top row: W Edwards (Caretaker), Gomer Morgan (Borough Accountant), T Williams (Rate Collector), W R Hall (Librarian).

2nd row: Councillors Enoch Davies, Llew Samuel, Captain Bertie Taylor Lloyd M C, Major George Fossett Roberts OBE, Major Abraham Thomas (Medical Officer), Captain Edward Llewellin, Rees Jones (Borough Surveyor).

3rd row: Canon Williams (Mayor's Chaplain), Councillors David Ellis, Professor Edward Edwards, T J Morrison, Dr T D Harries, J Barclay Jenkins, Rufus Williams, David Davies, Rhys Jones, J D Williams, John Morgan.

Front row: Ald. Edwin Morris, Ald. J Evans, Ald. Daniel Thomas, Ald. E P Wynne and Mrs Wynne (Mayor and Mayoress), John Evans (Town Clerk), Captain Thomas Doughton, Ald. C M Williams, Ald. T J Samuel.

APPENDIX

Recruits, Casualties and Tribunal Members

I. Recruits

There are few official statistics on wartime activity in Ceredigion. Recruits from the county often enlisted in Carmarthen, Brecon or elsewhere and the numbers from individual counties were not recorded. However, rough estimates of the number of recruits can be made using several methods (all open to anomalies), two of which are explained below.

In 1911 the population for Ceredigion was 59,879, with 26,918 being males. Rounding up the figures, the population was about 60,000, with about 27,000 males, of whom about 11,000 were aged between 18 and 51 and therefore eligible to serve at some point during the war.

i) According to one source – I F W Beckett, *First World War: Essential Guide to Sources in the National Archives* (2002), p.121 – the percentage of the male population that served in the armed forces in Britain was 22.1%. If the total male population of Ceredigion was about 27,000, then about **6,000** males served. However, as a relatively high percentage of the male population of the county was employed in agriculture, and in general more recruits were enlisted from urban areas, this is likely to be an overestimate.

ii) By extrapolating data from the West Wales Memorial Project, I estimate that about 684 males **resident** in the county were killed during the war. This includes merchant seamen, but excludes those who were identified as living outside the county (e.g. it has been claimed that the first Aberystwyth soldier to be killed was my great-uncle, Ivor Christmas Phillips, who died at the battle of Aubers Ridge in May 1915, but he had left Aberystwyth for London with his family as a small child and is consequently excluded from these statistics, despite his name appearing on the Aberystwyth war memorial). Some war memorials and rolls of honour in the county record the names of recruits as well as those killed. 16 of these record 128 deaths from the total of 955 who served, a percentage death rate of 13.4%. If the total number of deaths for the county is 684, a 13.4% death rate would suggest that **5,104** served.

The average of these two figures is about **5,550**. If this number of men served out of the total of about 11,000 eligible men in the county, it means that about half served and almost half did not. Those who did not included farmers, some farmhands and others considered to be undertaking work essential to the war effort, those who failed a medical, together with a handful of conscientious objectors. The number of women who served is more difficult to estimate.

II. Monthly Casualty Rates

The number of monthly deaths for the county can be seen on the Ceredigion Archives' website (https://ww1ceredigion. wordpress.com/colledigion-ceredigion-1914-1918-ceredigion-war-casualties-1914-1918/), which shows how the death rate varied from month to month. The graph below, based on this data, is very revealing. Apart from the peaks in July 1916 (notably as a result of the battle for Mametz Wood) and in some months of 1917, as well as during the German offensive in the spring of 1918, the death rate was at its highest in the last months of the war (August to October 1918), when battles were fought in the open as the Allies attacked the Hindenburg line and other German defences.

Ceredigion

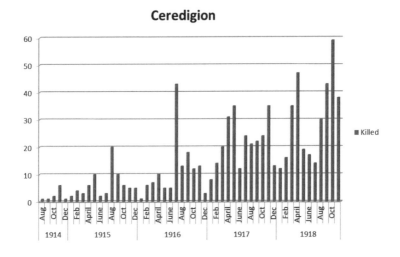

III. Members Of The Cardiganshire County Military Tribunal, 1916–1918

Listed below are the names of those who served on the County Military Tribunal, together with some information relating to them. The following comments are based on this information.

- There were 11 members (in general, all were present at each session of the Tribunal).
- There were no women.
- There were no representatives of the working class (it should be noted that as the members were unpaid, apart from expenses, and as most meetings were held during the daytime, the majority of the working population were thus precluded from being able to serve).
- The average age of the members (in 1916) was 55/56.

- There were six Anglicans and five Nonconformists (although about eight out of ten of the population of the county were Nonconformists).
- Eight (or possibly nine) of the members could speak Welsh, with three (or two) unable to do so (about nine out of ten of the population of the county could speak Welsh).
- There were six Liberals and four Conservatives (with the one unknown probably also being a Conservative).
- There were four farmers; three businessmen; two in the legal profession; one minister of religion; one of independent means.
- Seven of the eleven were county councillors.

John Jones JP of Cwmere, Felinfach (Chair); farmer; county councillor; Liberal; Welsh speaker; Nonconformist (Independent); age (in 1916): 62/63

Evan Evans of Aberystwyth (Clerk); solicitor; Liberal; Welsh speaker; Nonconformist (Presbyterian); age (in 1916): 65/66

Joseph Evans JP of Llanfair Fawr, near Lampeter; farmer; county councillor; Conservative; Welsh speaker; Anglican; age (in 1916): 50/51

Sir Lawrence Hugh Jenkins of Cilbronnau near Cardigan; lawyer (formerly Chief Justice of Calcutta); Conservative; Welsh speaker (possibly); Anglican; age (in 1916): 59/60

Evan Lima Jones JP of Aberaeron; chemist and optician; county councillor; Liberal; Welsh speaker; Nonconformist (Presbyterian); age (in 1916): 61/62

R J R Loxdale of Castle Hill, Llanilar; estate proprietor; county councillor; Liberal; non-Welsh speaker; Anglican; age (in 1916): 56/57

R R Nancarrow of Pontrhydygroes; lead mine manager and mining engineer; political allegiance unknown (probably Conservative); non-Welsh speaker; Anglican; age (in 1916): 31/32

D C Roberts JP of Aberystwyth; timber merchant; county councillor; Liberal; Welsh speaker; Nonconformist (Presbyterian); age (in 1916): 66/67

R S Rowland JP of Garth, Llanio Road, Llanddewi Brefi; farmer; county councillor; Conservative; Welsh speaker; Anglican; age (in 1916): 47/48

Herbert M Vaughan JP of Plas Llangoedmor; High Sheriff of the county and man of letters; Conservative; non-Welsh speaker; Anglican; age (in 1916): 45/46

The Revd John Williams JP of Cardigan; Baptist minister; county councillor; Liberal; Welsh speaker; Nonconformist (Baptist); age (in 1916): 66/67

Sources

General

Most of the primary sources used for this book are to be found at the National Library of Wales (NLW) or Archifdy Ceredigion Archives (CA).

Many of the most useful sources I have used have been digitised, including material from all the archive services in Wales, as well as the NLW, which were available on the Cymru1914 website. Unfortunately, this website is no longer functioning. The NLW website includes the following explanation (May 2021): 'The Cymru1914.org website is unavailable due to technical difficulties and the National Library of Wales no longer has resources needed to redevelop and maintain the website. We are currently looking at other ways of giving access to collections that were digitised by the project and of redirecting existing links to the relevant collections. If you have any questions regarding the website or its content, please contact the NLW Enquiries Service.'

I have made extensive use of the Welsh Newspapers Online site (https://newspapers.library.wales/www), which is free for anyone to access – unlike British Newspapers Online, which is behind a paywall.

The Welsh Newspapers Online site includes digitised copies of *The Cambrian News* for the war period but, frustratingly, *The Welsh Gazette* only covers the period up to and including 1910, while the *Cardigan and Tivy-Side Advertiser (C&TA)* was not part of this digitisation project. These newspapers are all available on microfilm at NLW. Hard copies of the *C&TA* are held by CA and a limited index is available. I do not provide individual references to newspaper sources in the chapter sources below, as they are readily accessible by searching the Welsh Newspapers Online site.

The four volumes of *The Aberystwyth War Book* at NLW, largely compiled by Margaret Powell Evans of Penparcau, contain not only press cuttings but some documents relating to the local war effort.

The West Wales Memorial Project (https://www.wwwmp.co.uk/ceredigion-memorials/) provides valuable information on war memorials and members of the armed services from Ceredigion killed in the war.

Biographical information on some individuals mentioned in the text is to be found in the *Dictionary of Welsh Biography* (available free online: www.https://biography.wales/).

A good overview of sources and interpretations of the war relating to Wales is to be found in Paul O'Leary, 'Wales and the First World War: Themes and Debates', *Cylchgrawn Hanes Cymru | Welsh History Review*, vol. 28, no. 4, pp.591–617.

The most useful general publications consulted include:

Ifor ap Glyn, *Lleisiau'r Rhyfel Mawr* (Llanrwst, 2008)

Robin Barlow, *Wales and World War One* (Llandysul, 2014)

Mike Benbough-Jackson, *Cardiganshire: a concise history* (Cardiff, 2007)

Cofio'r Rhyfel Mawr: WW1 Remembered 1914–1918 [bilingual booklet published to coincide with an exhibition arranged by North Ceredigion Free Churches in 2014] (Aberystwyth, 2014)

Richard van Emden & Steve Humphries, *All Quiet on the Home Front* (London, 2003)

Aled Eurig, *Gwrthwynebwyr Cydwybodol yn y Rhyfel Mawr* (Llanrwst, 2018)

Michael Freeman, *Conscientious Objectors in Cardiganshire during the First World War*, (Aberystwyth, no date [*c*.2014])

Adrian Gregory, *The Last Great War: British Society and the First World War* (Cambridge, 2008)

Peter Hart, *The Great War* (London, 2013)

Gwyn Jenkins, *Cymry'r Rhyfel Byd Cyntaf* (Tal-y-bont, 2014)

Gwyn Jenkins & Gareth William Jones, *Cymru a'r Rhyfel Byd Cyntaf* (Tal-y-bont, 2015)

Angela V John (ed.), *Our Mothers' Land* (Cardiff, 2011)

Gil Jones and David Steeds, *Aberystwyth Town FC: Fallen Heroes of the Great War* (Aberystwyth, 2014)

W J Lewis, *Born on a Perilous Rock* (Aberystwyth, 1980)

Arthur Marwick, *The Deluge* (London, 1967)

Gerald Morgan, *Ceredigion: A Wealth of History* (Llandysul, 2005)

Catriona Pennell, *A Kingdom United* (Oxford, 2012)

William Troughton, *Aberystwyth and the Great War* (Stroud, 2015)

Chapters

I

For the data on church and chapel membership, see *The Royal Commission on the Church of England and Other Religious Bodies in Wales and Monmouthshire: Report of the Commission*, published in 1910. For census data on the Welsh language (1911), see *British Parliamentary Papers*, 1913, lxxix (Cd.6911) 885. For the golf club dispute see NLW Dr B G Charles Research Papers: Aberystwyth Golf Club, and R J Rees's diary 1912 (NLW ex 2564). For further references to Rees, see Chapter IV. For Henry Richard, see Gwyn Griffiths, *Henry Richard: Apostle of Peace and Welsh Patriot* (London, 2012). The diarist was John Jones, Royal Oak, Taliesin, whose diary was published in part in *Lloffion Llangynfelyn*, 4, 1957. The statistics for the membership of the Cardiganshire Battery is based on the list published by William Troughton in *Aberystwyth and the Great War* (Stroud, 2015).

II

The photographs were published in Howard C Jones, *Aberystwyth Yesterday* (Barry, 1980). I am grateful to the author for his permission to include them in this book, and for the information on Dick Arfon Jones. For Dafydd Jones, Llanddewi Brefi, see NLW MS 23269E, and for William Jones-Edwards, see his autobiography, *Ar Lethrau Ffair Rhos* (Aberystwyth, 1963).There are a number of chapel histories, the most useful being Brynley F Roberts, *Cyfannu'r Rhwyg: Hanes Eglwys Salem Aberystwyth 1893–1988* (Caernarfon, 1995); Mary Brown, *English Methodism in Aberystwyth 1869–1969* (Aberystwyth, 1969); and Moelwyn I Williams, *Y Tabernacl Aberystwyth 1785–1985* (Aberystwyth, 1986). For the Revd Moelwyn Hughes, see his *Pregethau* (Birkenhead, 1925). I am grateful to Martin Edwards for providing me with a copy of the letter from Dr T D Harries. Other relevant publications include: Harri Parri, *Gwn Glan a Beibl Budr: John Williams, Brynsiencyn, a'r Rhyfel Mawr* (Caernarfon, 2014); D Densil Morgan, *The Span of the Cross: Christian Religion and Society in Wales 1914–2000* (Cardiff, 1999); D Densil Morgan, 'Christ and the War', *Journal of Welsh Religious History*, 5, 1917, pp.73–91. The letters from Rifleman Willie Stanley Jones were published in part in the local press but the original letters are to be found in the NLW Aberystwyth Comforts Fund Papers, 1914–19, together with many other letters from those at the front.

III

The events of October 1914 are well covered by the Welsh press and also by some English newspapers, including *The Daily Telegraph*. Contemporary references are to be found in the diaries of T Gwynn Jones and R J Rees (see Chapter IV), the Aberystwyth Council School log book, 15 October 1914 (CA), and in *The Dragon*, May 1916. The status of Mrs Ethé and Mrs Schott's nationality was the result of the British Nationality and Status of Aliens Act, passed in August 1914 (http://www.legislation.gov.uk/ukpga/Geo5/4-5/17/enacted). Details on Professor Schott's family and Bill Morgan's imprisonment in 1888 are to be found through searches on www.Ancestry.co.uk. More recent accounts of the events are to be found in E L Ellis, *The University College of Wales, Aberystwyth, 1872–1972* (Cardiff, 1972); R T Jenkins *Edrych yn ôl* (Denbigh, 1968); and Tegwyn Jones, 'Erlid yn Aber', *Essays and Poems presented to Daniel Huws*, ed. Tegwyn Jones & E B Fryde (Aberystwyth, 1994). See also Panikos Panayi, 'Anti-German Riots in London', *German History*, VII, issue 2, 1 April 1989, pp.184–203. The story about the alleged spy was related to me by Mr Terry Edwards.

IV

All the main sources for this chapter are at NLW: R J Rees's diaries, 1905, 1912–1942, (NLW ex 2564) and T Gwynn Jones's journal (T Gwynn Jones papers D293). There is also information in R J Rees's scrapbook (CMA 22844) and Morgan Rees's letters (CMA 23075-23147); and in the T Gwynn Jones papers, including some correspondence between the two, together with interesting correspondence between Jones and the journalist E Morgan Humphreys. There is no biography of R J Rees, although an article on him by Ieuan I Phillips appears in William Morris (ed.) *Deg o Enwogion* (Caernarfon, 1965). The autobiographical works by his son, Goronwy Rees, contain some details about him – see John Harris (ed.) *Sketches in Autobiography* (Cardiff, 2001) – as well as in the biographies of him: Jenny Rees, *Looking for Mr Nobody: The Secret Life of Goronwy Rees* (London, 1994) and John Harris, *Goronwy Rees* (Cardiff, 2001). There are two Welsh-language biographies of T Gwynn Jones: David Jenkins, *Thomas Gwynn Jones: Cofiant* (Denbigh, 1973), and Alan Llwyd, *Byd Gwynn – Cofiant T. Gwynn*

Jones 1871–1949 (Barddas, 2019). See also *Y Traethodydd*, April 1993; *Y Llenor*, 1950; *Y Cymro*, 24 September 1919.

V

The ditty appeared in *The Carmarthen Journal* (28 January 1916) and the *Brecon County Times* (3 February 1916). Contemporary sources include: Cardiganshire Agricultural Executive Committee and the Cultivation sub-committee minute book, 1917–21 (NLW Minor Deposit 939); NLW Edgar Chappell Papers D1 and D2; Edgar Chappell 'Wages and Conditions of Employment in Agriculture in Wales.' 1918, Cmd. 24, vol 1; *The Welsh Outlook*, June 1918.

See also: David Jenkins, *The Agricultural Community of South-West Wales at the turn of the Twentieth Century* (Cardiff, 1971); David A Pretty, *The Rural Revolt that Failed: Farm Workers' Trade Unions in Wales, 1889–1950* (Cardiff, 1989); A W Ashby and I L Evans, *The Agriculture of Wales* (Cardiff, 1944); J M Davies, *O Gwmpas Pumlumon* (Aberystwyth, 1966); William Jones-Edwards, *Ar Lethrau Ffair Rhos* (Aberystwyth, 1963); Caroline Dakers, *The Countryside at War 1914–18* (London, 1987); Peter Dewey, *British Agriculture in the First World War* (London, 2014); Gareth W Williams, 'The Disenchantment of the World: Innovation, Crisis and Change in Cardiganshire, c.1880–1910', *Ceredigion* IX no. 4, pp.303–321; David Howell, 'Labour Organization among Agricultural Workers, 1872–1921', *Welsh History Review*, XVI, pp.63–92; David A Pretty, *'Gwrthryfel y gweithwyr gwledig yng Ngheredigion 1889–1950'*, *Ceredigion*, XI, I, pp.41–58; Bonnie White, 'Feeding the war effort: agricultural experiences in First World War Devon, 1914–17', *Agricultural History Review*, 58, I, pp.95–112; and Gwyn Jenkins, *'Locustiaid Ceredigion'*, *Papur Pawb*, 156 & 158, 1990.

VI

Few records of the Military Service Tribunals in the UK have survived (see https://www.nationalarchives.gov.uk/wp-content/uploads/2016/02/Military-Service-Tribunal-survey-Dec-2015-copy.pdf) as the Government ordered their destruction after the war. However, the records of the Cardiganshire County (Appeals) Tribunal were kept at the office of its Secretary Evan Evans, and subsequently deposited at NLW. The applications for exemption case documents have since been digitised and can be accessed on the NLW website: www.library.wales/discover/digital-gallery/archives/cardiganshire-great-war-tribunal-appeals-records . I am grateful to staff from the NLW for access to the underlying database for this project, which allowed me to extract some useful statistics. The information provided in press reports varies, with some reports including the names of individual appellants while others omit them. Files of correspondence and papers kept by the agricultural representative on the County Tribunal, J H Davies, are to be found among the NLW Cwrt Mawr papers S8–S10. The article by County Tribunal member H M Vaughan, 'The Cardiganshire Appeal Tribunal' was published in *Wales* 1947 no.25, pp.171–180.

See also: James McDermott, *British Military Service Tribunals 1916–1918* (Manchester, 2011); David Littlewood, *Military Service Tribunals and Boards in the Great War* (London, 2017); Robert Phillips *'Gorfodaeth Filwrol yn sir Gaerfyrddin yn ystod y Rhyfel Mawr'* (unpublished University of Wales, Lampeter thesis, 2007); Robin Barlow 'Aspects of the Great War in Carmarthenshire' (unpublished University of Wales, Lampeter thesis, 2000).

VII

The story of David Evans, Cribyn was related in '*Cymru 1919*', a radio programme broadcast on BBC Radio Cymru on 17 November 2019. For David Morris Jones, see Gerwyn Morgan, *Beulah: The story of a Ceredigion village and its people* (Cardigan, 2016), pp.333–4. For W H K Owen, see Gwyn Jenkins, *Cymry'r Rhyfel Byd Cyntaf* (Tal-y-bont, 2014), pp.102–3. For Dafydd Jones, Llanddewi Brefi, see NLW MS 23269E. For 'Mami Siencyn', see William Jones-Edwards, *Ar Lethrau Ffair Rhos* (Aberystwyth, 1963), p.68. For Rachel Davies, see Enid Gruffudd, *Llythyron Rhyfel fy Mamgu*, (privately printed, Tal-y-bont, 2019). The information on Gwen Stephen was obtained from *Cymry 1914–1918*, a radio programme broadcast on BBC Radio Cymru, 5 November 1918. For Emilie Evans, Gwenllian Evans, Beryl Morgan, Sophie Rowlands, Nesta Morgan, Maud Jepson, and the Ddarllenfa Sewing Circle, see the NLW Aberystwyth War Book, vols. I–IV.

VIII

Log books for the county's schools are held by CA. They vary in content depending on the approach of the head; some provide only basic information, such as attendance statistics, but others include details on events and activities. There are also some published histories of schools. The most useful of these, for the purpose of this chapter, were: Kate Davies and T Llew Jones, *Canrif o addysg gynradd: Hanes Ysgol Tregroes, 1878–1978*, (Llandysul, 1978); *Dathlu Canmlwyddiant Ysgol Gynradd Cwrtnewydd 1878–1978 / Centenary Celebrations, Cwrtnewydd Primary School* (1978); Huw Spencer Lloyd, *History of Aberystwyth County School (Ardwyn) 1896–1973* (Aberystwyth, 1996). The Welsh Department of the Board of Education's H.M.S.O. publications include: *Dydd Gŵyl Dewi (St David's Day)* (London, 1914); *Dydd Gŵyl Dewi (St David's Day)* (London, 1915); *Patriotism: Suggestions to Local Education Authorities and teachers in Wales regarding the teaching of patriotism* (London,1916). See also: Programmes of the St David's Day celebrations held in various schools in Wales, 1916 (NLW Misc. Records 562). For Daniel J Davies, see *Cymry'r Rhyfel Byd Cyntaf*, pp.124–5 and Michael Freeman, *Conscientious Objectors in Cardiganshire during the First World War*, pp.10–14. For T Bryn Jones see *Y Darian*, 1 May 1919 and Ysgol Tregroes school log book (CA/TRG/2). For a general history of the experiences of schools during the war, see Barry Blades, *Roll of Honour: Schooling & the Great War, 1914–19* (Barnsley, 2015).

IX

For T E Nicholas, see Hefin Wyn, *Ar Drywydd Niclas y Glais* (Tal-y-bont, 2017); David W Howell, *Nicholas of Glais: The People's Champion* (Clydach, 1991); T E Nicholas '*Dros eich Gwlad*' (NLW D M Jones Collection); and for his articles on the war see *The Merthyr Pioneer*. The infamous Inglis-Jones letter is to be seen in '*Niclas a'r Heddlu Cudd*', *Bro*, *Rhagfyr* 1979, pp.29–30. For John Fitzwilliams, see NLW Cilgwyn Estate Papers; I have mostly relied on the papers relating to Major John Fitzwilliams MC 1914–1918 accumulated by Alan N Owen (NLW ex 2725) and also his articles published in *Carmarthenshire Life*, 2007–2009. For Sir Terence Keyes, see Richard Wittingham, *Terence Keyes: Imperial Disguises* (Oxford, 2019); see also Michael Occleshaw, *Dances in Deep Shadows: The Clandestine War in Russia 1917–20* (London, 2006).

X

For the Welsh inmates at Ruhleben Camp, see *Cymry'r Rhyfel Byd Cyntaf*, pp.177–8. I am grateful for the information on D J Evans provided by his grandson John Evans; to Howard C Jones for the information on his uncle, David John Jones; to Aneurin Jones, Lampeter, for information about his father John Jones, Dihewyd; and to Gilbert Jones for the information on Alf Jenkins. For Evan J Jones, see the file on those from the Aberbanc area who served in the two world wars compiled by John T Jenkins (NLW ex 1739). For Richard Jones and J L Jones, see NLW Cwrt Mawr papers S9. For Willie Evans, Hafod, Nantcwnlle, see 'A Short History of the Parish of Nantcwnlle', paragraph 56, published on the Genuki website https://www.genuki.org.uk/big/wal/CGN/Nancwnlle/HanesNantcwnlle. For the University graduation ceremony, see H M Vaughan, *Wales* 1947 no.25, pp.171–180. For George Maitland Lloyd Davies, see Jen Llewellyn, *Pilgrim of Peace* (Tal-y-bont, 2016). For ex-soldiers' organisations, see CA: ADX/119/68-69: Minute Book, Aberystwyth branch of the Welsh National Federation of Discharged and Demobilised Soldiers and Sailors, 1919–1924; British Legion: Aberystwyth Minute Books 1925–32, 1932–34. For the county's war memorials, see Angela Gaffney 'The Great War in Wales: memory and monuments', *Ceredigion* Vol. 14, no. 1 (2001), pp.137–156. For Mario Rutelli and the Aberystwyth War Memorial, see https://pilgrim.ceredigion.gov.uk/index.cfm?articleid=7898. For the history of Cardigan Hospital, see http://www.glen-johnson.co.uk/cardigan-priory-hospital/. I'd like to thank my old friend Geraint Roberts for information on his uncle, David Samuel Roberts, and to Dinah Jones for information on the Cribyn area. The J M Davies and William Jones-Edwards autobiographies are referred to above. The John Davies interview was published in *Llafar Gwlad*, 30, 1990, pp.20–1. The quote by Margaret Macmillan is to be found in *The War that Ended Peace* (London, 2014), p.605.

Index

By the same author:

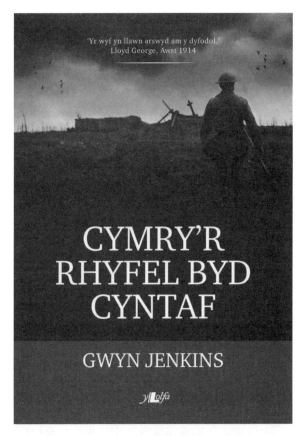

'Yr wyf yn llawn arswyd am y dyfodol.'
Lloyd George, Awst 1914

CYMRY'R RHYFEL BYD CYNTAF

GWYN JENKINS

y Lolfa

£9.95

Perhaps the definitive history of the First World War from
the Welsh perspective, recording the experiences of
soldiers, sailors, nurses, munitionettes, pacifists and
many others from all over the country.

Also from Y Lolfa:

£12.99

The story of the horrific First World War battle
for Mametz Wood in July 1916, including personal
accounts from soldiers on both sides and photographs
published for the first time.

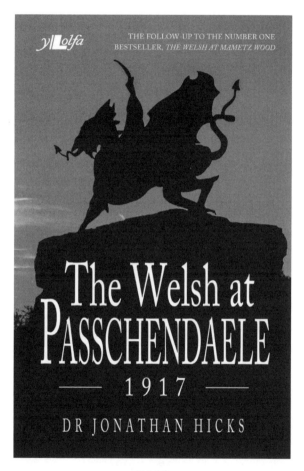

THE FOLLOW-UP TO THE NUMBER ONE
BESTSELLER, *THE WELSH AT MAMETZ WOOD*

The Welsh at
PASSCHENDAELE
—— 1917 ——

DR JONATHAN HICKS

£14.99

A detailed study of the Welsh soldiers who fought in 1917
at Passchendaele, where hundreds of thousands were killed
or wounded. It brings together poignant stories of personal
experiences and previously unpublished photographs.